PANNING
FOR
GOLD

PANNING
FOR
GOLD

RECLAIMING RESPECT IN
TODAY'S WORKPLACE

ALLISON GRAHAM ANDERSON

MERACK

Published and distributed by Merack Publishing
California, USA

Library of Congress Control Number: 2024917130
Anderson, Allison Graham
Panning for Gold: Reclaiming Respect in Today's Workplace
ISBN: 978-1-957048-26-0 (Paperback)
ISBN: 978-1-957048-40-6 (Casebound)

To all of the assholes who I have worked with,
or almost worked with…mahalo!

.

CONTENTS

INTRODUCTION

America's workforce is eroding. The basic principles of human relationships are falling away like boulders, crashing from the cliffside into the frothy ocean waters below. Current working environments now exhibit a shocking absence of respect, empathy, and understanding. In today's workplace, treating each other as we would want to be treated has fallen by the wayside. These issues are not new and have been in existence for some time now, but they have heightened drastically over the past decade. COVID-19 played a huge part in fast-tracking the loss of fundamental principles including respect, empathy, and understanding. This loss has caused a cavernous divide between our leaders and the rest of us who work for them leaving us with divided workplaces that can feel like hellish nightmares.

If you are like me, I'm sure you have experienced the "Sunday night scaries" and not wanting the weekend to end, or just the thought of having to walk into your office another day making a pit in your stomach. I've been there, and I am sure a good number of you have as well. When I speak of these hellish nightmares, I'm talking about organizations that make you feel those things. These workplaces could be described as toxic workplaces, devoid of respect, that do not give you the space to talk or think for yourself, let alone value things like diversity and equity.

Respect, empathy, and an overall understanding of others yield a happy, productive, and successful workplace where people want to contribute and have a positive impact on the organization. This successful relationship dynamic results in more profitability for the company with happier shareholders, customers, and workers. Being talked down to, treated like a child, and micromanaged takes workers in the other direction in which they will do just the bare minimum required and stick their middle fingers up as you leave the room. I would know—I have done this (a lot; seriously, an immense amount of times).

The purpose of this book is to explore the working relationships between leadership and everyone else, in an effort to make our workplaces productive, profitable, and overall enjoyable for everyone involved. The focus is on the dynamic between our leaders (or Gold Bars) and those of us who work for them (Gold Nuggets). The stories and examples I share are a result of over twenty years of bullshit via working in Human Resources. So, "you're welcome" in advance for this walk down HR memory lane.

GOLD NUGGETS AND GOLD BARS

Before we explore the stories of my work, I need to formally introduce you to the two stars of this read: my Gold Bars and my Gold Nuggets.

With my career built in science spanning over twenty years in primarily biotech and biopharma, we are definitely heading to the periodic table of elements for inspiration and explanation. I was a science lover long before it was cool and long before shows like *The Big Bang Theory* existed and made it okay. Gold (or Au) has an atomic number of 79 and is a transition metal. Like people, this metal has been around since ancient times. Again, like people, we grade and rank the metal. With gold, like people, some are difficult to extract and distribute, while others operate much more easily.

For the purpose of this book and subsequent examples, we are going to generalize our employees via Gold Bars and Gold Nuggets. Gold Bars will summarize our executives and our leadership, while Gold Nuggets will represent our younger and newer workers within the current workforce.

Do not jump to any conclusions assuming prioritization over one or the other. Neither will be placed on a pedestal but instead used as reference in an explanation of what has broken down with our workforce, what each is looking for, and what they each bring to the table. Our Gold Bars are fewer in number when compared with our Gold Nuggets, and while not necessarily better than our Nuggets, they certainly are the ones controlling our workplaces.

As you think about Bars versus Nuggets, I need to remind you about gold purity. This is where the true value is derived, not always based on size alone. For example, 24-karat gold is much more pure than 10-karat gold. So, within the parameters of this book, do not judge all of the value based on the size alone, but consider with that the purity of our Bars and Nuggets, and that is where our story forms.

Gold Bars do not just exist; they are created and formed through extreme heat, time, and processing. As the Nuggets struggle through early work experiences, they face the heat, but this alone does not turn them into bars of gold. With real gold nuggets, it often takes several passes through the heat to remove all the impurities of other metals and debris that may be contained within. This is also true of our human Gold Nuggets, as they will generally also take several passes through life and work experiences to be formed into those Gold Bars.

Throughout this book, we will look through the flames of the fire to find lessons both Gold Bars and Gold Nuggets attain. We'll use this insight to improve our hellish workplaces and examine how we can reintroduce the basic concepts of respect, empathy, and understanding. The hope is the re-creation of happy work lives paired with successful, productive, and enjoyable work environments.

SATAN'S CIRCUS

To set the tone for this book, we'll begin our story at none other than Satan's Circus. That's right, a girl who is completely and utterly afraid of clowns of any kind will begin in the fiery hell that we will from here out refer to as Satan's Circus. It's not your typical circus—it's actually a workplace. Set during the COVID-19 pandemic and run by the largest group of fiery asshole clowns you will ever see. While these experiences were not always pleasant, they are valuable in painting a picture.

I lived in Southern California for over twenty years and primarily spent my working days in the biotech industry, either working in or running the Human Resources function. While my job requires me to be outgoing and very verbose, I have always struggled with panic and anxiety going back to high school days. I need to set this story by telling you that all of the COVID-19 bullshit and living in a state that had an egotistical, hypocritical governor increased my panic and anxiety tenfold. And that might even be an understatement of the impact it had.

There were not many mental health programs or resources for what I would consider an average person like myself. The programs in existence at this time were generally directed toward the unhoused, people with children, and those with higher levels of medical necessity. I'm just a normal, middle-aged, somewhat functioning person. From the outside I would fathom a guess that you couldn't even tell there was anything chaotic going on in my head, but I feel it necessary to provide you with this background to help with the understanding of my state of mind at the time. Perhaps like me, you felt that simply leaving the house post-pandemic was an enormous feat of strength. And so, when interviewing with Satan's Circus, you can understand why I was immensely clear about how I wanted to be able to work remotely at least a couple of days a week. You might be able to relate when I say that working from home put me at ease, provided a support pet, and just overall comfort. It made me happy. Even stressful meetings or intolerable days felt more manageable from home versus being in the office.

Throughout the interview process I was assured that this hybrid working condition was feasible, and even agreed to by my direct Gold Bar (a.k.a. boss). However, as I would soon learn, this promise of, "Absolutely, you can work remotely a couple of days a week" quickly transformed into, "We need you in the office every day." It was about two months into my new job when I received the mandate of being required to now be present in the office five days a week…no ifs, ands, or buts.

Even prior to this mandate, I cried almost always on my drive to work. I lived about thirteen miles away, but with traffic, the commute was often at least an hour. During the height of the pandemic time, traffic was almost nonexistent, but that was a temporary reprieve. With my stress and anxiety of having to drive into the office, some days I had to pull over on the highway because I could not see through my tears. There were also days that I prayed for the horrid traffic to return as it would provide more breathing time. But alas, in the pandemic heights, the traffic was not there to support me, so on those really rough days I either pulled over on the freeway or cried in the parking lot at work prior to walking in.

It was not my job, nor the Gold Bars and Nuggets who I was working with, that brought on my tears. It was simply the exercise of leaving my home, my safe space, and going into the unknown. At this time, we did not have vaccinations, we did not know fully how or what was transmitted, nor did we know in what manner. We had folks constantly getting sick and needing to quarantine, but we did not yet have access to home tests then either. It was all a medical gamble when you just sat there and waited for your cough to start or your throat to burn. And this was why I had been happy with the hybrid working schedule. At least I still had some days where I was able to work from home, and I did not have to deal with the added stress of being in the office and what it may expose me to.

It was on one of these fine days when I was required to be in the office that my Gold Bar decided to visit our office location. Corporate headquarters was in a different city up north. Headquarters was drivable, but definitely not "pop-in-able." As she greeted me in the parking lot, I still had my sunglasses on. She had no idea I had just spent ten minutes on the side of the highway trying to get my shit together. An unexpected visit from my Gold Bar certainly didn't help—it just added another level of anxiety and an overwhelming sense of dread. While I was likely not in the best mental space, I still managed to smile and start the day's conversation. I thought, "Maybe I'm overreacting and this won't be so bad."

As she approached me in the parking lot, there was no small talk at all. She immediately began talking about requiring all employees to return to the office. I insisted that going from zero to sixty, and bringing people back five days a week would be upsetting for many. I wanted to offer advanced notice of the changes coming and a titration period where folks adjusted to two or maybe three days and then increased from there. Further considering: childcare, possible parent care, or maybe even car sharing.

My case was similar as I had no notice whatsoever. I was told on a Tuesday that from there on, I would be required to be in the office five days a week. End of story. It was an absolute living hell.

My insistence for my fellow Gold Nuggets and Bars gave way to my following comment: "We need to be respectful of employees' time adjusting and needing to care for family, travel logistics, and other similar aspects."

My Gold Bar: "If they don't like it, they can leave. They should be grateful we selected them and allowed them to work here."

My Gold Bar insinuated that they—Satan's Circus—had done us all a favor by selecting us to work for them. And sadly, this is not an exaggeration of what was said, nor is it paraphrasing. These are the exact words, and they clearly demonstrate the intent and lack of utter respect underneath those words.

The conversation further continued, "They should have their kids in daycare anyway, so there should be no need to arrange for childcare."

I quickly shared my personal experiences and how it was difficult even for me with no childcare or parental care concerns. I again reiterated that I did not prefer to be in the office five days a week, to which I was again told, "You should be lucky we allow you to work here."

Again, those words are verbatim. You literally could not make this shit up.

A piece of me died inside as a result of this conversation. My Gold Bar's comments were a dagger to the heart. I was already struggling with my mental health because of my anxiety and lack of confidence, and now I was being taken down even more pegs with one short conversation in a parking lot. From my perspective, this conversation and way of thinking was blatant disrespect. A disrespect not only for my mental health and safety, but also my work and company contributions.

My jaw dropped. I don't believe I said many, if any, words for at least a couple of hours. I was floored. What kind of crazy, ass-backward world did I fall into? On some level, I felt this was my fault as this hot bunch of ass clowns showed their colors on my first day, and in my stubbornness to make things work and/or lie in the bed that I had made, I stayed.

Flashback to noon on my first day of working there. Despite COVID-19, my HR Gold Bar had traveled to our office location and took one of the two local Gold Bars out to lunch. I was not bothered or offended by this; with COVID-19 in full effect, I was more than happy to sit in my window-less, cave-like office with the door shut knowing I was at least safe from disease in there. Just a few minutes go by before a list-all email was sent out by the company President, and head Gold Bar. Within this email, he informed us that the other local Gold Bar, a C-suite executive (this is HR lingo for Chief level officers like a CEO or CFO) was no longer with the company. Ummm, what? I will also tell you that this C-suite executive Gold Bar was just in his office not even twenty minutes ago, and we even had a meeting planned for that same afternoon.

The entire business unit was running around like chickens with no heads, wondering what had happened. Most of these headless chickens were solidly pissed and looking to me, HR, for the answers. Sadly, I had zero answers and about three dozen questions myself. I explained to the employees who were brave enough to come and ask me that I had no information and only questions myself.

About thirty minutes after the email was sent and the chaos ensued, my direct Gold Bar and another local Gold Bar came back from their lunch. I quickly pulled my boss aside and asked if they had known and/or heard the news of what happened. My Gold Bar's response…"Of course, that's why I wanted to take the one remaining local Gold Bar out to lunch. I wanted to explain and let her know." I was absolutely stunned.

They had gone out to have an executive lunch and talk about the monumental impact this change would have on our local business unit, and meanwhile I was trapped in the asylum with the inmates who were all absolutely pissed. The bulk of these Gold Nuggets and Bars had taken their jobs because of that C-suite executive Gold Bar. Now, that Gold Bar was gone. And this was all coincidentally happening on their new HR person's first day. Yeah, that would be me. What an amazing way to make an impact and gain the trust of your new coworkers.

Thankfully, at least from my side, the business unit quickly learned that this betrayal and lack of communication had nothing to do with my arrival and everything to do with the company's culture overall. I spent about twenty minutes after this happened on the phone with the recruiter who had placed me there, balling my eyes out. I remember pacing back and forth on the same block in front of our office building for what felt like an eternity. I didn't know where to go or what to do. My exact words on repeat with her were, "What the fuck did I just do?" I was experienced enough to know what these actions meant for the overall culture. These were not red flags—they were the equivalent of football fields filled with red flags. I should have left the Circus then and there.

I share all of this to explain and lay the foundation of just how fucked up relationships, working or personal, can be without the existence of respect and empathy. Without a basic understanding of what others might think or need. Employees living in silo existences negatively impact their working environment.

This book is not solely about Satan's Circus, even though there are a lot of amazing examples spewing out of those experiences to help prove my point. Respect and empathy yield a dynamic, successful working relationship that fosters productivity and happiness in the workplace. Sadly, Satan's Circus was not one of those places. However, I'm happy to report that companies that hold values in respect, understanding, and similar traits do exist. And at the end of the day, I am grateful for all of the experiences, both positive and negative, for without them, this book would not have been possible.

THE REALITY

As employees and as humans, we deserve more and we deserve better. Together we have the ability to shift the dynamic and be part of a joyful and healthy workplace. Everyone, regardless of their Gold level status, years of experience, and job function, deserve to be happy at work.

Throughout this book we will explore real-life examples of both the successes and failures that exist in our workplaces. It's with those examples that I provide strategies for relationship building, communication, understanding, and an overall feeling of connection and belongingness. Of course, you are also subject to my very East Coast directness and somewhat dark sense of humor, but this passes the time and the pages within.

It is with this awareness of our workplace challenges that we can begin to learn and change those behaviors. This will lead to positive environments bursting with flourishing relationships for all Gold Bars and Gold Nuggets. This existence benefits not just the individuals but their productivity, as well as the organization's profitability and overall success as well.

My greatest hope for you is that by reading this book, you will be able to curate a workplace culture where people feel excited to come to work and create magic together.

CHAPTER ONE

WHAT'S MEANT TO BE WILL FIND YOU

I am and have always been a reluctant leader. I do it and it comes naturally, but if you asked me about it or if I wanted it, I would most definitely say, "No."

With that, let's start our "herstory" lesson at a conference room table on the campus of Millersville University in "Bumblefuck," Pennsylvania.

I attended Millersville for my undergraduate studies and while there, pledged a sorority: Theta Phi Alpha. As I sat at the conference room table as a recent inductee of the sorority, I discovered that the long, arduous Sunday night meetings were the norm. Topping off this coma-inducing event, on this particular Sunday night we also had elections to vote for the sorority's Chairs and Officers for the next year. I will spare most of the details of this meeting as it would put me to sleep as well, but this snooze-fest of a meeting yielded a crucial turning point in my life regarding my future career.

My sisters (both pledge and otherwise) nominated me—yes, me—as Sister Spirit. This meant it was now going to a vote, and I was considered a viable candidate. I thought this was immensely off-base. Sister Sarcastic, or Sister Fuck No Way, I mean either of those (if they had existed) would have been a tremendous fit, but Sister Spirit? I detest Spirit and, even more on a basic level, humans…especially assholes. How in hell were they adding all of my least favorite things together and calling it my new job?

I was basically shitting myself at the table over the mere thought of this vote and what I would now have to do if I was elected for this position. The laughs around the table were deafening and honestly louder than the "nays" or "yeas" in the vote. I went numb for a bit and don't even recall hearing words for at least ten minutes. I think if I had followed in the former Orange President's footsteps and requested a recount, it would have just yielded even louder laughs and stronger smiles.

For those of you lucky enough to have bypassed the Greek world, Sister Spirit is a Chair position for a person who embodies the spark and passion of loving Greek life and our sorority. This is shown through hosting events, having themed activities, working with the Philanthropic Chair, and basically fostering and building relationships both internally as well as with other Greek chapters and outside community-based groups.

I wish I were joking when I tell you that I did not vote for myself, but alas, I'm not. In the end, I was elected and held the Sister Spirit Chair for multiple years. This, my dear reader, was the beginning of my Human Resources career. The lesson that I share with you here is that oftentimes in life, things choose us…we do not choose them. And what is meant to be, or who you are meant to be, will inevitably find its way to you.

FATE HAS OTHER PLANS

Just so you know, I still went out of my way to "unselect HR." My undergraduate degree is in Economics. My first job out of college was in communications for a non-profit in New Jersey. I was kind of dealing with people, but much more so data, writing, editing, etc., so this was awesome. Limited human interaction, if you will.

One day, I decided I would move to California—no job, no prospects, and I had never been there, so…. You're right, brilliant idea! Once arriving there, I took a temporary job with a global defense company and found myself in the Benefits group within an HR department. I was still seeking other opportunities. ("I'm soooo not an HR person," or so I thought.) I asked my Gold Bar (a.k.a. boss) to be a reference for me for a full-time opening in the purchasing department. In my inexperienced idiot mind, this was like shopping as a job, right? Well, I know enough now to know this was not the case, and obviously my Gold Bar was well aware of this too.

My Gold Bar was a sharp-tongued New Yorker who wore jeans every day. This Gold Bar provided me with an East Coast connectivity, and I was beyond comfortable with her. As far as language goes, the word "fuck" was as common as the word "the" and let's be honest…I was in love with this. So upon my asking for a reference, I was totally bummed when she told me no. But her reasoning for her response was much more compelling and went something like, "No way. You are HR. I'll make a job for you here."

And so she did. I was now officially working in HR.

It was at this juncture that a career spanning over twenty years began, encompassing a handful of organizations and thousands of employees. Human Resources and all of its glory came back to find me. This encounter had perfectly positioned me to take my new "office" as Sister Spirit of the ever-changing workplace. I was now entering a new world where I was a perpetual conduit between Gold Nuggets and Gold Bars.

CHAPTER TWO

GENERATIONAL AWARENESS

I need to start you with information on generational awareness as it touches every chapter throughout this book.

Today's workforce comprises the most working generations that we have ever had at one time. We currently have five generations spanning Gold Nuggets and Gold Bars from the ages of 16 through 75. This wide age range has caused some of the friction within our workplaces.

Generational differences in values, ethics, and overall in values, ethics, and overall workability have strained the tapestry of our workplaces, but, as you will see later in the book, it does not have to be that way. The philosophical deviations from generation to generation are vivid and have most definitely been felt or seen by all of us at one point or another in our workplaces.

For some background, we start with the Traditionalists who are pre-1945 and very much staying at their one job for the duration of their lives.

Next, we have our Baby Boomers, often referred to as Boomers, and they are the ones who taught us loyalty and the importance of work and values related to work. While we will see more job and company changes than we do with our Traditionalists, it's still minimal compared with other generations.

Gen X comes next and includes those individuals born from 1966-1977. This is where we start to see the proverbial foot coming off of the "work-first" gas pedal. While Gen X still partially identifies through work, it is more of a challenge than it was with the Boomers or Traditionalists. For the Boomers and Traditionalists, work was hard, and hard work was expected. With Gen X, we start to see a trend take place where work-life balance first comes into play, and they will make job changes more freely.

Following Gen X are the Millennials. This is the first generation to take their foot completely off the "work-first" gas pedal. In fact, they like the brakes. In this generation we see much more desire for freedom and flexibility. They want to change jobs and will do so at any point. Work-life balance is not a desire, it's a necessity.

Next we move to Gen Z, which encompasses those who were born between 1995 and 2010, and make up one of the youngest generations in today's workforce. Our Gen Z Bars and Nuggets favor happiness and take into account their own mental health. They do not define themselves through their work as we see with our Baby Boomers and even some of us born thereafter who followed in those footsteps.

Both Boomers and some of us Gen X'ers identify ourselves primarily through our working hours and not by our lives or happiness. Part of the holy grail that our Gen Z's are after is flexibility within their work schedule and a sense of purpose, with these factors weighing more for our Gen Z's than an annual salary. Again, polar opposite from our Boomers and even X'ers like myself.

A survey by Adobe, "The Future of Time," found that 66% of our Gen Z Bars and Nuggets would switch jobs for more control over their work schedules.[1] If we add this to our "You MUST be in the office" Gold Bar temper tantrum, you end up losing a workforce. They will find consultant-based projects or similar, they will stay at home with the parents, and in short, they will not yield to this juggernaut temper tantrum. They will simply walk away.

So, what does this mean for the rest of the workers?

I'm going to dig into my friends and family on this one. For many of those other workers, inclusive of both Boomers and some of us Gen X'ers, they are checking off calendar

21

days. Do they like the ridiculous mandates that sometimes come from our workplaces? No. But are they going to fight them? Not likely. Therefore, a lot of our current Boomer and Gen X'ers, both Gold Bars and Nuggets, are simply biding their time. Even with my own family members and some former colleague Gold Nuggets and Bars, they are working from their own presumed timetables. I can't tell you how many times I hear, "Just two more years of this shit." Or, "I only have three more years to go." And so, they put their heads down and abide by their employer's requests. They are waiting for those magical calendar pages to fly off the wall until they see their targeted escape date, or quitting date. And as far as productivity and engagement? You are shit fuck lucky if you're getting 40% of their capabilities out of them on a regular basis. (Sorry, Mom and Uncle Nasty!)

CHAPTER THREE

GOLD BARS

As a reminder, for the purpose of this book, our leaders, C-suite folks, and executives will be referred to as "Gold Bars." Depending on the size of the organization, you may even think of a Director or Senior Director as being at that Gold Bar level. These are folks who have put in a ton of time, have been to hell and back through their experiences, and can successfully lead a group of people regardless of the industry or organization type we are discussing.

For those of you not as familiar with the HR vernacular, let me introduce you. C-suites are the President, Chief Executive Officer, Chief Operating Officer, Chief Financial Officer, and the list goes on. When I speak of C-suites, it's literally any of the titles beginning with a "Chief" designation. Generally reporting into the C-suites, you will see Vice Presidents, possibly Sr. Vice Presidents, and similar. More commonly in smaller organizations, you will see Director and Senior Director level folks also directly reporting into the C-suites. Within the context of this book, I would likely consider all of these folks to be Gold Bars.

While the bulk of my experience lies within biotech and biopharma, a lot of these companies are smaller and generally exist with a few hundred employees or less. Regardless of the size of an organization, these Gold Bars are solidly running the show. One advantage to working with a smaller company is that you are able to dig in more in this "all hands on deck" type of environment. That closeness offers you more interaction time with the Gold Bars, assuming this is something that's attractive to you.

In my experience I have seen where this level of interaction is really gratifying for some Gold Nuggets, as they are able to directly communicate with the Gold Bars and feel like they are making a direct impact on the organization. It provides a space for the Gold Nuggets to etch their initials in that still-wet sidewalk cement for decades to view once hardened. While that is true for some Nuggets, we obviously have others who prefer to camouflage themselves into the surroundings and do not necessarily want that direct contact time with the Gold Bars. These Nuggets prefer to fly under the radar. And for what it's worth, our Gold Bars will need both types of Nuggets to run a successful organization.

DIFFERENT TYPES OF KNOWLEDGE

Our Gold Bars generally bring a wealth of industry experience and skills to the table. Let's be real—they are not functioning as a Chief officer of anything without having laid the groundwork and put a shit-ton of time into their craft. Yes, I will say that some have solidly bullshitted their way to the position, and we will certainly see a few assholes as well, but the truth always has a way of revealing itself. Bullshit will only take you so far for so long, and good employees, regardless of Bar or Nugget status, will not work for an asshole forever. They will tire of the drama and unnecessary stress and opt for a more human Gold Bar, searching for one who more closely resembles themselves and offers respect and understanding in the workplace.

I can speak specifically about the Gold Bars within the biotech and biopharma space. These Gold Bars have seen success, but sadly there is often more failure than success in our industry. Biotech and biopharma is an industry of losers. The amount of drugs, devices, and compounds that do not receive approval or ever get to market is approximately 9 out of 10 drugs.[2] That's right, we are unicorn hunters in this business. And let's add even more drama to the "Real Drug-Makers of California" reality show that is biotech…it takes about twelve years to bring that one unicorn drug to market and on average costs approximately $314 million to do so.[3]

Our industry is built on drug failures. However, this is not a bad thing, folks. This is what added to the weight and purity of the Gold Bars by providing life lessons that molded and shaped their experiences and who they are. Lessons learned and then later avoided provide a better shot at hunting that elusive unicorn compound. There is no other way to learn these lessons, and for this reason alone, we need to respect our Gold Bars.

An example of my level of respect for Gold Bars within my industry comes from a personal experience within education. I don't believe anyone is ever done learning, or should not be at least. I share this story as it has greatly impacted me, and just a fair warning, I'm going to be throwing Harvard under the bus with this one. You can laugh now…it's expected.

I was accepted into a summer executive program at Harvard regarding healthcare in the U.S. Honestly, I was beyond thrilled to be accepted to a school like Harvard. In addition, my job was so supportive of this wild tangent of mine. I could not have asked for more. Throughout the lessons, we explored the life cycle of healthcare, discussing every aspect and player in the game. As you can imagine, this topic has so many moving parts, and it is my goal not to put you to sleep with a sidebar, so with that I will cut to the chase. In the section on biotechs, pharmaceutical companies, and medical device companies, the instructors were very data/numeric driven. With this, they were instructing that the industry overall needs to reduce prices and provide free medications, free devices, and more. That we, as an industry, are charging too much and not supporting those in need.

What these instructors failed to see, failed to ever experience, is the sheer volume of companies in our industry that have to close their doors, lay everyone off, and/or sell off other drug or device assets just to pay the rent for one month. They did not lecture on this. Nor did they look at the number of years, blood, sweat, and tears (literally, folks!) that went into each month and year of the life of this drug or device's life. They did not look at the money—all of the money on both direct and indirect drug or device costs—that went into just getting one (hopefully a unicorn) drug to clinical trials, let alone all the way to market. Nor did they ever mention the costs that we pay to federal agencies as part of this approval process.

I'm not here to lecture on United States healthcare, as there are already enough books causing narcolepsy on the market, but I am here to explain how immensely valuable these lessons are. And no matter how incredible that teacher or institution is, it can never be compared to real-life experience. It's like trying to compare apples to frozen fish sticks. We're not even in the same grocery aisle at this point. These experiences and life lessons of our Gold Bars can never be duplicated and have made them who they are today. Both successes and failures alike.

I think sometimes it's hard for our younger generations to understand just how much work and sacrifice was put into life for these Gold Bars. The world was a very different place forty, even twenty, years ago for working folks. Things like loyalty and patience played a huge part in working.

These Gold Bars (mostly Nuggets at the time) were just forming and were accepting of what was presented to them. They were happy for a two% raise, as it was two% more for their family or their household. Loyalty was hugely valued, and they put their heads down to do what they needed to for their organization and their families. An argument with a supervisor or not agreeing with a new vice president was just a bad day at the office—it was not a reason to quit or look elsewhere. Getting something like a "Meets Needs" or a 3.5 out of 5 on a performance review rating was expected. They did not quit, or write to HR about how disappointed they were in the review or amount of increase they received, because they did not get a "Far Exceeds Expectations," or a 5 out of 5. They understood that not everyone would be an executive. They knew it was only *la crème de la crème* and not a path for all who wanted it, but instead a path for a select few.

Some of our Gold Bars belong to generations where their family lived through trying times like the Great Depression and World War II. Even more migrated to the United States with little or nothing and had to climb their way to a safe and stable life for themselves and their families. These experiences shaped how they value things like employment, providing for family, and an overall respect for those in leadership roles. These are traits that are not seen in younger generations, and these are experiences they can only imagine or read about. These hard-fought values and experiences no longer exist and have fallen by the wayside.

A large number of Gold Bars with similar experiences to the ones described above are still in our workforces and running the show out there. Those experiences have molded these Gold Bars very distinctly with strong work ethics, a sense of morals, and loyalty to the organization and Board of Directors. Our Gold Bars are hard-wired this way, and sometimes this yields a disconnect with the Gold Nuggets who do not share the same level of values, morals, loyalty, and overall work ethic.

This level of "living knowledge" is priceless and cannot be duplicated without living through these experiences ourselves. We must honor and respect those lessons and the knowledge that our Gold Bars bring with them. They are our workplace historians, able to tell the stories because they have lived them. Take for example my telling you a story because I read a book about it, versus me sharing my life story with you. We all know which one is going to leave a larger impact, and it's definitely not my recollection of the latest Stephen King thriller I read. When there's heart, passion, and true interest, that conversation or story is captivating and emotional. Think about grandmas or historians and how much love, passion, and insight they add to their stories. That sense of heart and emotion you feel is just not able to be manufactured, no matter how someone might try. For this, our Gold Bars are an absolute wealth of knowledge and experience. I have learned so much from the Gold Bars throughout my career and continue to do so daily. And I would go further to say that anyone reading this should also take advantage of their information wealth and knowledge while we still have it in our workplaces.

A DISCONNECT

As I hinted at in an earlier paragraph, this also leads to what can be a disconnect between the Gold Bars and Gold Nuggets. While understanding and having first-hand experience with their own generation and experiences, they both also need to show respect and understanding for those who are different. Having one set of experiences, challenges, and background is not better or worse in any way, but just different. Our Gold Bars did not "have it easy" in any sense and have certainly earned their Gold Bar status. However, they still need to support and be open to those coming from different backgrounds, experiences, and generations. In some cases, this is much easier said than done.

An example of this comes from a recent interview that I was on. I was meeting with the organization's Gold Bars, and the position I was interviewing for was that of a leader in HR for their organization. They had been having a hard time finding the right fit for their role, and while I found that hard to believe at first, it was understandable after my in-person meetings with their Gold Bars. The timing of these interviews was post-COVID and followed the loss of my father. Because of those two huge, life-changing events, my one working desire was a remote position so that if and when shit hit the fan again, I was able to do my work and also support my family by being present. As you have read by now, this was certainly the opposite case from that of my last employer, and so it was now a non-negotiable item for me and at the very top of my new employer "wish list."

Like a lot of others in the job market post-COVID, having some aspect of a hybrid working model was the first item I brought to the attention of the recruiter when they called to ask if I wanted to discuss an opening they were looking to fill. Sometimes, stating the ability to work remotely was the very first line of my email. I am not alone in this desire, and I know from helping others on the other side of employment searches, we all have our reasons for wanting that flexibility. I'm also in full support of those folks who want and need to be present in the office five days a week. To each, their own.

I was as clear as a bell with my recruiter that my bottom line ask was for a minimum of two days a week of being able to work remotely. In my head this would provide me with a long weekend should I need to help out back East with my family, or be able to visit when my nephew was in town. As we went through approximately thirteen in-person interviews (I wish this were an exaggeration), I encountered both Gold Nuggets and Bars on both sides of this remote wall. Some were very clear to say that it was five days in the office, while others would say the job was flexible and they were working remotely here and there.

I was untrusting with this mixed bag, as I had just come from a workplace where in at least a dozen interviews I heard, "Sure, we will not require you to be in the office 100%." Further in the process, "Yes, almost everyone is working from home periodically. We completely understand." And again, "We can definitely accommodate working from home at least two times a week." Yet, this was not even close to the case as it was mandated that I must be physically in the office five days a week, whether I liked it or not. Five days a week whether I had a car or not. So you can see my PTSD at play with a murky mixed bag of viewpoints on a hybrid working environment when I had already had the wool pulled over my eyes at the last place.

My first interview with the Goldest of Bars did not even enter into a space where we would get into the nitty-gritty of the workday or week. It was a high-level overview where we were looking at the forest and not any specific trees. This is common, especially in my line of work. Finding jobs is like fitting puzzle pieces: it can't just fit on one or two sides, it has to fit all the way around. So this was a standard meeting. During this in-person interview, I met with at least ten other Gold Nuggets and Bars. All went well, and this was then followed up by another on-site interview invitation to meet with the Goldest of Bars again.

Unlike our last meeting, this time we did dive into the nitty-gritty of all of the specific tree types in the forest. Upon the Gold Bar's asking for my first question, it was that of a remote ability. "How do you work with your team on remote work and flexibility?" The Gold Bar simply said, "There is no remote ability. This position is five days a week in the office and critical to do so at that. This remoteness that people are looking for is fleeting and will fall by the wayside." He continued, "They will be the ones to lose out and will not have jobs when they need them because they chose to be remote." Upon further discussion I found out that the HR leader they had previously hired had left the company for an opportunity that was fully remote. For the former HR leader, as it was shared with me, the need was for flexibility with her children, and remote working offered that ability. Regardless of the reasoning, I understood this.

As you can imagine, at this point I have, in my mind, wasted days' and even weeks' worth of time on all of the interviews, on-site visits, research, etc. Just to have it come crashing down in one simple response. "There is no remote ability." There was also no respect or understanding for what folks were dealing with or had in their personal lives. If you are respectful and understand that there may be more than one way of doing something, you open an entirely new world. I'm not saying that my way is correct, but what I know beyond a shadow of a doubt is that for me, right now in my life, I need that remote ability. I will never again almost lose out on seeing a parent or loved one because I work for a controlling, untrusting bunch of asshole Gold Bars.

At the crux of this inability to see any way besides this Gold Bar's way of thinking is an inherent lack of respect and an untrusting person. Believe in your team, believe in the over twenty years of HR experience that I would have brought to the table, and trust me to put in the time and effort, regardless of what that may be to get the job done. Respect my wishes and current place in life that brings me to these needs. I'm not saying that my beliefs should be the only beliefs, but respect my experiences and wishes with understanding that for myself and my family, this is a non-negotiable for me. As you can imagine, this was the end of the process for me, and I did not go further with them.

A part of me understands this Gold Bar's thought process and workplace desires. But I will not work in an environment where respect and understanding are not mutual. That relationship would maybe last a year or two if I could hang in that long, or did not experience another major life curveball. And although I have respect and understanding for that Bar's side, I also very much disagree with remote work ending anytime soon. For those of us who were forced back into it, five days a week regardless of our level, job, or working hours, that re-entry was difficult. I know without a doubt that I will never go back to a situation where physically in an office five days a week is a requirement. Those days are done, at least for this Nugget-like Bar.

I share my story as a direct representation of the general consensus that we currently see regarding the desire for a hybrid working model in today's workplace. At least the majority of workers prefer that flexibility. A study by LinkedIn shared that nine out of ten workers preferred to work remotely. While this might sound a bit high, most studies yield somewhere around 70% of workers looking to work remotely or having the flexibility to do so. A study shows that only 12% of workers, including both Gold Bars and Nuggets, prefer to work in the office five days a week.[4] This is definitely placing my story in the majority and not the minority and thus representative of a new shift in working trends, despite the belief of some Gold Bars.

I also share this story as a prime example of needing and understanding mutual respect for differing points of view in the workplace. Whether this differing opinion is Gold Bar to Bar or Gold Bar to Nugget is inconsequential. It's the overall premise of mutual respect for varying points of view, and each has their place at the table. This was nonexistent within the organization's culture whereI was interviewing in the prior story. And in my case, a hard pass when it came to making my next career move.

CHAPTER FOUR

GOLD NUGGETS

When talking about the "Gold Nuggets," I'm speaking of those folks who are generally newer to the workforce, or "green," as well as the folks who are in the entry phase of their tour into management. These are individuals who can and will impact the organization but are not the ones who are currently running it. There should be no more value placed on Bars versus Nuggets, or vice versa. Everyone adds value and at the end of the day is a collaborative, respectful, diverse team that gets the job done.

When we look at the newer generations, who are mainly Nuggets at this point, we must examine their composition. They are a completely different breed when compared with the older generations like myself and those who came before me as well. Our Nuggets value an overall experience, they want to be part of the bigger picture, they want to make the world a better place but make no mistakes, and they also want a Vice President title and pay despite the minimal years of experience they bring. What is unique about them is that they are not afraid to quit without all of the above-listed items. Living at home with the parents is standard at the age of thirty, and they're not afraid of it. Back in my day, when we left for college, we never looked back. We did whatever necessary to scrape enough money together so we did not have to move back home with our parents. And if we look at even older generations before Generation X, some of them flew from the nest even prior to that time.

One of the most amazing attributes of our Nuggets is their desire to make the world a better place. Our Gold Nuggets value human life and experience like no other generation before. They want to be part of the solution, and their drive and desire for diversity comes naturally. These are areas where our Gold Bars need to learn and listen from the Gold Nuggets. Generally speaking, these items and viewpoints are not inherent to our Gold Bars. Diversity is the perfect example of this.

When we look at diversity, most of the Gold Bars will verbally tell you that they support it, but have you ever asked them to define it? The responses you receive might be entertaining, but sadly they are not always on point. Today's Gold Nuggets are asking the Gold Bars to "talk the talk" and "walk the walk."

Again, not all responses to this request fail and some even flourish, but within today's workforce we still have Gold Bars who believe that diversity is obtained by hiring one black person and taking a one-hour online class. Make no mistakes, this is not the answer to obtaining diversity, nor would this fit the definition of operating as a diverse organization. As for today's Gold Nuggets, they know this and are on top of it.

DIVERSITY NEEDS DIALOGUE

Let me give you an example. I was approached to interview for a company that was very "diversity forward," at least in their communications. However, my first step is to always research the company and look to see the composition of the leaders. Interestingly, the definition of diversity does not include a leadership team composed of all white, middle-aged males. I was not impressed, and while I entertained the initial conversation, I could easily tell there was no interest in truly correcting or changing their special brand of diversity. I did not go further into the interview process with them.

Our Gold Nuggets know and respect that diversity is not a solo objective. They also inherently know that this encompasses inclusion, equity, and belongingness. Within my past experiences, I had a very telling encounter with two of my Gold Bars and one Gold Nugget. Whether I wanted to or not, I eventually became the middleman on this one. I do not hesitate to say that COVID-19 and everything we all dealt with during those initial months and years has taken a massive toll on our mental health. Let's add to this outside forces and scary things that seem to be happening daily now. In this particular case, one of my Gold Nuggets was having a hard time handling everything that was going on in her life. As a young Asian female living on her own, the Asian hate crimes that were happening during quarantine in and around the areas where we lived, Southern California, were just adding to an already full plate. She was struggling with everything and shared this information with her boss. He was one of the amazing Gold Bars and was confident in the fact that he knew what he knew, and he knew what he didn't know. As a white, male Gold Bar, he knew that the life crisis she was experiencing was not his forte and told her she might want to reach out to HR.

This is where HR came into play, but at this time it was not me. Our conflicted Gold Nugget had reached out to a fellow Gold Nugget who was also Asian, close to her age, and worked in HR. Perfect fit, right? She seemed to think so as well, and felt that by reaching out to someone who was her age and also an Asian female, they would better understand how and what she was feeling. Much to her surprise, she was told that work is not the place to talk about things like this, and work was just for work. This is not the response you should ever receive from anyone in HR, Nugget or Bar.

Some time went by after this conversation before our amazing Gold Bar urged his Gold Nugget to try someone else, and this would be where I entered the conversation. I had come to find out that it was not only this one interaction, but at another point our Gold Nugget had tried to share this with the lead Gold Bar who is also female and within her department. Instead of listening, providing empathy and understanding, she also told our conflicted Gold Nugget that work was for work and nothing else. Furthermore, she told her that she needed to leave those feelings at home and they were not to be brought into the workplace.

Learning of this from our Gold Nugget, I was absolutely floored. I had truly admired this lead Gold Bar and was very surprised by her reaction to our troubled Nugget. In some respects, this felt surreal to me. I would never have expected that approach and utter empathetic neglect from such a trusted and valued Gold Bar. Much to my surprise, this approach only got worse when I had to share the status and situation with my HR Gold Bar. It was a proverbial kicking in the teeth as my own Gold Bar boss also believed work was not the place for such talk, and she was pissed at me for even spending time trying to make our Gold Nugget feel better. Further, my Gold Bar believed I was wasting both of our time by even bringing this situation up with her. Like some of the others, this Gold Bar's opinion was also that our troubled Gold Nugget needed to discuss these things at home with family, or get a friend or a therapist.

I cannot stress enough how upset our Gold Nugget was by the events going on, COVID-19 lockdowns, and just life in general at this point. It takes an excessive amount of stressors to bring an employee—Nugget or Bar—to share these feelings and ask for help. It absolutely broke my heart that she had made multiple attempts at finding support and was met time and time again with no compassion, no outlets, and instead a dismissal of her feelings, emotions, and cries for help.

This is wrong on a million levels, and at the end of the day, regardless of who you are or what you do, you have the right to feel comfortable, understood, and accepted for who you are and how you feel. Every human is different, and there are no two of us who are painted or created in the exact same way, and that is okay. It's actually more than okay—it's quite amazing and provides us with such a diversely rich tapestry. And our Nuggets, they get this concept lock, stock, and barrel. They thrive on this, and they need this within their workplaces to be successful. Gold Nuggets and Gold Bars as well need to be, and deserve to be, in environments where this is celebrated, respected, and encouraged.

Sad to say, it took a long time before I was able to mentally reach these Bars and explain just how critical this is to all employees, Nuggets or Bars. While they listened to me, I knew they still did not agree and were just giving me the space to air these words so I would finally leave them alone about it. I am convinced that if you asked, even today, they would still not get it or give half a shit about it.

In a lot of cases, this is not about being fully onboard with things, but at least listening, respecting, and understanding where our Bars and Nuggets are coming from. I will never have the same fears as my Gold Nugget as I'm not a young Asian female, but I can still listen, show respect, and provide her with the empathy, understanding, and safe space she deserves.

As an interesting aside related to this case, within the organization and around the time that all of this was transpiring, I had been setting up a Diversity and Inclusion training. While I did not initially receive approval for all staff to attend, the first two sessions were for the vice presidents and above. So, all of these folks in the initial training were Gold Bars. I will also tell you that the instructor, who is an absolutely brilliant lawyer, is a Gold Bar, PhD, black male, and one of the best speakers on topics in this area.

I have worked with this Gold Bar speaker for over twenty years through various companies and organizations. He has a very informative and interactive way of getting his point across, and as a black male going into lots of heavily white companies, industries, and executive board rooms, his real-life stories are beyond captivating. Because I had worked with him for so many years, I knew his position and also knew my Gold Bars were in desperate need of his knowledge and the facts that were behind them. Completely unprovoked and with absolutely no knowledge of what we had going on with my Gold Nugget, he walked the class through a scenario very similar to what we had been working on. His explanation detailed the obligations of an employer and our Gold Bars to provide a safe, healthy workplace where everyone feels comfortable and that they all belong. I could not have said it better myself but also knew after the meeting how my Gold Bars would likely still be dismissive of these messages.

I know we cannot make all horses drink the water no matter how many times we lead them down to it, but I would definitely say that I had expected way more from those Gold Bars given the presentation's depth, information, and facts behind it. At this point, I knew they would never get it and that their workforce, which has seen a tremendous amount of turnover, would continue to do so until they have some Gold Bars in that mix who understand and help make the necessary changes. In this particular case, I'm happy to report that our distressed Gold Nugget found her way to a new company where she was valued, understood, and respected.

FUTURE GOLD BARS

By not working with our Gold Nuggets now, we are not building leaders and Gold Bars for the future. This is critical as we all know these experiences are key. Our Gold Nuggets are not staying in jobs where they do not feel respected, heard, and valued. They are leaving—they are fine with working consulting projects and piecing together jobs from A, B, and C Company. They do not mind living at home longer as they are not willing to compromise those values.

According to the McKinsey & Company study called the American Opportunity Survey, when looking at the younger generations, we see trends where they are more likely to have multiple jobs, and over 51% of those in Generation Z (born between 1997 and 2012) do independent work like consulting versus having a standard, in-house, 9 a.m.–5 p.m. job.[5] If we are to compare this with all other generations, we only have 36% working independently—and we've even got the old timers or partially retired Nuggets and Bars in that category.

We need to find a way to come together so we have and are building future resources who can successfully take the Gold Bars places tomorrow and thereafter. The experiences and skills you gain from consulting projects or similar are not even close to the knowledge learned first-hand day in and day out. The ups and downs experienced is what adds the most value, and this is where we grow as leaders, regardless of what our day-to-day tasks may entail.

Without understanding and working with our Gold Nuggets, we are also losing their perspective. While there is no true right or wrong, both opinions need to be listened to and heard. Gold Bars can learn so much from adapting and bringing in some innovative ideas and values that the Gold Nuggets hold so dear. We can make the world a better place by implementing some of the Gold Nugget ideas and suggestions. And let's also not forget the following: While Gold Bars may have been successful with a certain method or procedure at one or more points in their time, it doesn't mean we can't look at a Gold Nugget's method or procedure.

Generally, in my experience, it's usually a hybrid of the two that makes the most successful ventures.

WE'RE ALL SO STUBBORN

On another note, our Gold Nuggets tend to be as stubborn as our Gold Bars. With this, we yield a workforce conflict. The differences we encounter have a lot to do with the varying generations and all of their very different life experiences. It's this level of stubbornness where the commonality lies.

There was a point in my career when I was doing consulting work, predominantly in the not-for-profit space. These are generally smaller organizations attempting to do amazing things by making the world a better place, while operating on very limited budgets. They also tend to have a younger staff made up of lots of Gold Nuggets and maybe a couple of Gold Bars, if you are lucky. Budgets are not forgiving, and these not-for-profit organizations cannot just make or sell another widget to yield more money coming through their door. They have to rely on donations, grants, and similar fundraising mechanisms to achieve their missions.

With one particular not-for-profit, I had one Gold Bar and at least one dozen Gold Nuggets running the show for a very important cause. They were butting heads constantly and could not figure out how to combat the disagreement. I met with the Gold Bar and suggested a training presentation to the entire team (her included) on generational differences.

She agreed, and so into their offices I went to hopefully shed some light, and diffuse some of the negativity that existed as a result of their constant state of conflict.

This was my first time in front of this organization as a whole, and I was honestly not sure what kind of reception or response I would get. Now mind you, I know when presenting at any time and place that I get at least one asshole. They are common, and that's okay. Much to my surprise, this group was amazing, and their responsiveness was unlike anything I had ever expected or experienced. I didn't even have a token asshole in my class. They were brilliant students, wanting and craving this information. The training was successful and improved the organization's culture and performance.

FINDING APPRECIATION

In this case, the concept of having multiple generations working in one office producing multiple ways of working had escaped them all. A lack of respect was evident on the side of the Gold Nuggets as well as the Gold Bar. Sharing facts and information about each generation that is currently in our workforce, and the preferred ways they have of working, was an immense "a-ha" moment for all participants. The Gold Nuggets assumed the Gold Bar was being dismissive, and the Gold Bar was assuming the Gold Nuggets were just lazy. When in fact what we had was a stalemate because neither side understood how or why the other acted the way they did. We're going to dig more into this bucket of fun in a later chapter.

A lot of detail was provided on the "why" behind generations working in one manner or another and how this had come to be. By truly educating everyone and not just saying *X works like this and Y works like that*, they were finally given the full picture versus just one section or color. Weeks later, I was still getting notes and emails from them about how much more sense the Gold Bar's actions made, even down to her word choices. I will also say that while I felt my Gold Nuggets were beyond receptive, I did not get that same vibe from my Gold Bar. She was still in what felt like an entitlement phase where she was 100% right. This piece took more time and likely encompassed more areas such as needing to control all aspects of life, but at least this was a point to start the dialogue and begin to move things forward.

This also opened the door for direct communication with myself and the Gold Nuggets where they met me, understood me, and felt more comfortable with me. While this was great, this also ended up leading to a situation where they told me about some just solidly fucked behavior on the part of the Gold Bar. This situation itself warrants an entirely new book, but what I can say with certainty is that with education and information, our Gold Nuggets were more respectful, understanding, and better listeners, yielding a much more productive and happier workplace for everyone.

Building these bridges between our Gold Bars and our Gold Nuggets is imperative to be able to achieve a workplace of respect, empathy, and understanding—yielding a dynamic, successful working relationship, which fosters productivity and happiness for all who are part of it. You do not have to physically or otherwise experience something in order to respect or understand it. You just need to be present and listen, and in some cases take action to correct inequities. Regardless, all Gold Bars and Nuggets alike deserve a safe and comfortable workplace.

CHAPTER FIVE

CHANGING TIMES

I have spent literal decades of time, energy, and tears in the front row of the shit show we know as our workplaces.

My spot was generally sitting in the middle of whatever dumpster fire crossed by my desk that day. The problems always contained the same basic elements: the dumpster fire itself, with Gold Bars on one side and Gold Nuggets on the other, both yelling about who started the fire, but no one taking action to extinguish the flames. Given my time and experiences with this vantage point, I just can't sit back and watch further deterioration. I know there is a better way of doing business. I know there is a better and more respectful way of treating humans. And I also know that by reversing this degradation, we can positively impact the output, outreach, and productivity within our businesses.

We currently have a fundamental lack of respect. While many of us feel this disrespect in multiple facets of our society, the one place I can speak to emphatically with examples and knowledge is in the workplace.

Our workplaces are experiencing an epic tug-of-war for control between our Gold Nuggets and our Gold Bars, with neither side giving way and both sides believing they are in the right. Why? Lack of respect. Respect is missing on both sides. All of our golden treasures (regardless of composition or makeup) bring with them knowledge, experience, and vision for how they believe things ought to be and what they want to be part of. But neither side is willing to listen to the other. This lack of respect has yielded us a great disconnect between generations. In places where we need discussions and understanding, instead we are getting resignations, a stagnant workforce, memes, and gifs.

This problem is not new and has been bubbling under the surface for some time now. Our good friend COVID-19 threw gasoline on this and ignited it like nothing we have ever seen before. Think of volcanic activity and the movement and bubbling going on below the surface. With one good crack, shift, or quake, that shit is roaring hot magma regardless of the location and what might lie in its path. COVID-19 was the workforce's earthquake, and it shifted the ground enough to give that bubbling pressure cooker the space and opening it needed to explode. This explosion has yielded an insane amount of resignations and unhappy workers, as well as overinflated titles and salaries for a lot of the Nuggets and Bars who are still "willing to work." These issues did not happen overnight, and they will most certainly not be corrected overnight either. In fact, this is just the cusp of our volcanic activity—this is not even the aftermath or clean-up.

LET'S LOOK AT THE LANDSCAPE

When reviewing the past twenty years, the landscape that we currently work in as well as the composition of our workforce have greatly changed. We have more generations currently working in our workforce than ever before. Each of them brings a completely different set of experiences, values, and desires to the table. Also adding to this landscape is the addition of social media and the role technology now plays in all of our lives. This has had a massive impact on both the Gold Nuggets and Bars, as well as the companies themselves.

We also have to examine the sheer number of college graduates both at the undergraduate and graduate levels. This number has continued to increase over the past two decades as more Nuggets and Bars have become college-educated, bringing a stronger knowledge base to the workforce.

Finally, we can't talk about the differences between now and then without addressing probably one of the largest swings: the overall work environment. Corporate conformity has been replaced by a celebration of diversity and individuality.

Back when I began working, as a female I was expected to act and look a specific way. I had no choice in the matter and was literally evaluated for how I looked while performing my job. I recall one employer early in my career having a very specific dress code, and I was reprimanded for wearing what I was told was "casual beach wear." Okay, let's be honest here. I was making little to no money and shopped at the Gap as it fit my budget. And don't think I'm fancy, it was actually the Gap outlet. They had come out with a spring line of fun pastel-colored pants and tank tops, and I fell head-over-heels in love with what I viewed as a fun twist on work pants in the most subtle lavender color. And for what it's worth, I did put a white full-coverage sweater over my matching pants and tank.

I was told my clothes were unprofessional. I was also told that the size of my breasts was a running joke and regular commentary for the other departments. I was horrified, embarrassed, and just ashamed of myself for the things that were being said to me. Needless to say, with the limited work experience I had at this point, and needing my paycheck, I was not going to rock this boat again, so into the back of the closet went my "lavender lovies," never to see the light of day again.

Back in the day, you were "required" to dress in a very specific way for work. And sadly, a lot of those expectations were based on your gender. Not how you identified, but how those Gold Bars perceived you.

Now across the board, we tend to see more casual attire. But this new love and acceptance of work-leisure is not always a guarantee, and of course somewhat dependent on what your job is. And we also have space for self-expression, gender identity, and laws like the CROWN Act (stands for Create a Respectful and Open World for Natural Hair), which protect you from discrimination based on hairstyle or texture.

For office workers like myself as well as our scientists, it's definitely Business Casual Land. Everyone is an individual and somewhat respected or rewarded for that. So those conversations of the past because of my color choice or because there was too much cleavage under my sweater would not happen now. Or, if they did, I would happily sue the asses off. Not all of us live in black suits or pencil skirts, folks!

ONLINE OFFICES

Adding to this environmental swing, we uncover telecommuting and how much this has shifted our workplace. And this is me being reserved in my language, as "upheaval" is a more appropriate description post-COVID-19.

It is true that there have always been companies and positions where employees could work remotely, but these seemed to be exceptions to the case and a rarity in the working world. As we all know and have experienced, COVID-19 had different plans for us. The pandemic showed the literal world that a large number of us—especially office workers—were able to work from home. I have to say (at least in my experience), I was scared shitless of this at first. Maybe like me, you worked doubly as hard, or even triple that of your standard pace, immensely overcompensating in an effort to avoid hearing shit from your Gold Bars and/or proving to them beyond a shadow of a doubt that you were in fact putting all of your energy and time into your work.

Given my job and frequent interaction with my Gold Bars, I already knew that they were not supportive of a remote work environment. I had already tried like hell at multiple companies to get approvals for some medical writers and similar "individual contributor" type positions who actually required that space and quiet for their jobs. While some companies had already embraced this model, most did not. In my case, the attempts I had made for such positions were not generally success stories. Oftentimes, even after weeks of trying to prove my case, the best I could do was to negotiate a hybrid model for them. And I really need to emphasize the amount of effort in these cases so you understand how much of an uphill battle this was with our Gold Bars.

During those early days of the COVID-19 pandemic, working from home started as a challenge for me, as we would expect from any massive change in our daily routines. I went out of my way to work around the clock, was always available, always present, always using my camera, and through time I slowly began to love this lifestyle change. I would most definitely take care of myself to ensure I was presentable (at least of what the camera would capture), but I will tell you that what the camera did not capture were my most favorite pink UGG slippers and the softest sweats that ever existed from Vuori. These were just what the doctor ordered.

And I'm talking about immense benefits here…not even mentioning words like "commute" and how much time I had previously lost in my life on the I-5 freeway. Let's add to this the fact that a load of laundry could be thrown in over lunch and how beyond amazing it was to have so much quality time with my favorite beings on the planet—my furry monsters, Shadow and Thumper. Looking back at my journal, every day included expressions of gratitude for the kitties, for not having to endure a one-hour (or longer) commute each way, and for my joggers.

As individuals, learning such monumental lessons on the ability and benefits of telecommuting was huge! For some of us, this preference was unlike anything that had ever happened in our lifetimes, and while I know that this sentiment was not held by all, it was by the large majority of office workers. In a recent study (2024) captured by Forbes on Remote Working Statistics & Trends, a staggering 98% of the study respondents want to work remotely, at least part of the time.[6] The reasoning behind this is flexibility, autonomy, and a better work-life balance. This has been such a massive workplace shift, and while almost all of us fell in love with this concept, some of our Gold Bars are jaded by it.

AND THE VOLCANO BUBBLES

The environmental workplace changes I've just touched on have all added fuel to the magma fire of our workplace volcano, resulting in more intensity and heat.

While the focus is on the erosion of respect in the workplace, other factors have greatly contributed to this decline as well. We cannot entertain this conversation without mentioning the decades of 3% salary increases, which definitely added even more hot gasses to this molten volcano mix. When I was younger and newer to the workforce, that 3% was received only if you were lucky. And you did not question this increase. You took it, smiled, and then went home to bitch to friends and family about it. It almost became expected to have such a piss-poor increase, and lots of folks—both Gold Bars and Nuggets—did not want to push it or possibly lose that giant $40 per week increase. (After taxes, maybe $25 if you were lucky.) Don't get me wrong. I admit that $25 has saved some gas tanks, take-out dinners, forgotten bills, etc. But this less-than-stellar attempt at "thanks for busting your ass all year" did not make for happy, productive workers. It still doesn't today.

With all of these factors bubbling below the surface, all it took was one good COVID-19 quake, and that magma was flowing like none other.

That's where we currently are. We have fragmented our workforce. As a result of missing basic fundamentals like respect, empathy, and understanding, coupled with environmental factors that we have recently been dealing with, our workforce has cracked and shifted. Employees are no longer accepting a whopping 3% and smiling. They are no longer willing to sit like prisoners in office chairs five days a week. They are instead standing up for themselves and demanding more, or looking to find a new job that will provide it.

THE CRUX OF THE PROBLEM

I don't think anyone ever expected quarantine and COVID-19 to have such a lasting impact on our workforce.

In graduate school, I studied Public Health, and while we know that Public Health Emergency Declarations will not just disappear, I don't think any of us ever expected such highs and lows. Just looking at cases where they would "close the state" only a week later to "open the state" and then do it all over again a few months later brings us right back to the confusion and frustration we felt. Or if you were anything like me, we counted the days until salons and stores would open again, only to be devastated when the metrics changed and the window moved. The emotional impact was much more than most of us had expected. It was definitely nothing that I had ever learned in my graduate schoolwork or subsequent programs after. We had no playbook, handbook, or protocol for what COVID-19 brought into our lives on every level, including our workplaces.

An overwhelming number of both Gold Bars and Gold Nuggets left their jobs not long after our great COVID-19 quake. This time was appropriately labeled as "the Great Resignation." This was no joke, folks. For the first time in my lifetime and, honestly, decades before me as well, we had an outstanding number of Bars and Nuggets just quitting. The balancing of work and home responsibilities was too hard and did not work; people needed to homeschool the kids and take care of parents, and with all of that, they found they could save money in other areas. They already found they were saving money via much lower gas, food, childcare, and other costs. The great COVID-19 quake had offered an outstanding number of workers a way out.

I personally had several friends in this boat. Some had taken early retirements, some were spending extra time with kids and family, while yet others were exploring passion projects that had never before seen the light of day because of how busy they always were. Some opted for less of a working investment by consulting on a project or two.

I'm definitely not shy and will emphatically tell you that I will never step foot into an office again five days a week, fifty-two weeks a year. Those days are long gone for this Bar-ish Nugget.

We now have a tug-of-war where our Gold Bars want the workplace to go back to the way it was before when they were able to babysit us all, day in and day out. Our Gold

Nuggets are on the other side wanting at the very least to have a say in it.

We have our Gold Bars who are eager for asses back in seats like nothing ever changed, and our Gold Nuggets are saying, "hell no, we won't go."

THE GENERATIONAL DIVIDE

As you read in Chapter two, today's workforce consists of more generations working than we have ever seen before. This generational diversity brings with it many challenges that are new for all of us. For many Gold Bars, work has only ever existed as a physical establishment that you go to each day and do your job, and only your job. Their focus was on work and not on making friends, leaving a positive impact on society, or catching up on the latest episodes of a favorite Netflix show.

Today's Gold Nuggets are more of the latter. They are different in that they are looking for an all-encompassing experience. Yes, most certainly this entails getting work done, but it also includes things like connecting over coffee, planning a lunch run, or showing off a new haircut. In addition to social aspects, they want to ensure they are making a positive impact, both within society and local communities. These Gold Nuggets need to be heard, they need to have purpose, and they are not afraid to question things when any of this feels off. This is very different in comparison with many of our Gold Bars who have often led with the philosophy to not question their superiors, to get the work done, and to be loyal to their organization.

We also see a large difference in confidence and how this was obtained within our generations. A lot of Gold Bars from older generations gained confidence as a byproduct of decades of hard work and on-the-job experiences. You earned that space and respect through years and years of work. Our Gold Nuggets, on the other hand, have seemed to walk into our workspaces with little experience but a beaming smile and aura of confidence that follows their every move. These newer generations, where most of our Gold Nuggets are, have spent more time in school overall and automatically come equipped with the notion of how important they are to the workplace.

Recent trends show a large number of Gold Nuggets attending graduate school immediately following undergrad. They are taking and passing professional licensing exams straight from school as well. As a result, they are coming to the workplace with a much greater sense of confidence and, ironically, less practical working experience. In my opinion, this extended duration of their schooling, along with trends like providing trophies to second, eighth, tenth, and literally every place in sports and activities, has also added to this confidence phenomenon.

Confidence is most certainly a positive attribute regardless of how it is obtained. In the older generations, confidence came from decades of hard work and life experiences as compared with our newer generations where it seems to be almost automatic. This paradox of obtainment is enough to cause friction between the varying generations of our Gold Nuggets and our Gold Bars. It is our ability to objectively view and understand these generational variances that will enable us to use them positively in our workforces. Highlighting this diversity and using it as an educational lesson will better both our Gold Bars and our Gold Nuggets by each adopting some aspects from the alternative viewpoints.

A MENTAL HEALTH CRISIS

While our Gold Nuggets have been granted the immense gift of confidence, the irony is that they are more fragile at the core. Mental health has never before played such a leading role within our workplaces. Our world, as a whole, was taken aback by COVID-19, but the mental health impact of that was far greater.

A lot of us—including myself—suffer and have suffered from panic attacks and massive anxiety. Quarantine, television, and news with recent events triggered by race, politics, and global climate change have compounded that. For those with less traumatic experiences or life experiences (primarily our Gold Nuggets), this sense of loss and sadness was exacerbated during the past few years. In some cases, the bulk of their working time or adult life experiences happened during COVID-19, and they don't have as many other years of life lessons to draw upon. They only have this bleak, difficult time to use as a point of reference.

Mental health care and awareness need to play a much larger part in our workplace. There should not be a stigma surrounding mental health, and absolutely everyone deserves to be in a supportive culture with mental health awareness and management training, tools, and, at the very least, resources. Looking at organizations like The World Health Organization (WHO) and the Center for Disease Control (CDC), even pre-pandemic data shows that 71% of responding adults were or had experienced at least one stress-related symptom.[7] This was back when things were "good," folks. I shudder to think of the responses we would now see from a similar study.

I bring the area of mental health to the forefront as we need to address this head-on. Mental health directly impacts job performance and productivity. Its negative impact is also felt and seen via communications with coworkers, disengagement, and, in extreme cases, has even escalated to physical altercations within the workplace. Our Gold Bars need to understand how large of an issue this is and work to put tools and resources in place now to avoid even more resignations, employee burnout, and poor performance and productivity in the future.

As an HR professional, I can often sense when something is possibly going on with the employees. It's a bit of a superpower that we see within our profession. HR professionals witness withdrawal and differing behavioral patterns and usually see some verbal altercations with coworkers, Gold Bars, and even outside vendors. We walk a fine line at times—while we can ask if all is okay, or if they need anything, sadly it's when something truly happens in the witness of others before we can rightfully step in.

Some years back in a company long, long ago, I had a fellow Gold Nugget who was working in a department that I interacted with on a regular basis. We all reported to the same executive Gold Bar, so there was frequent interaction. I had noticed a shift in behavior, but at this time I was much more junior in my career and so I tip-toed around, asking if this person needed help or if there was anything I could do. Of course, "No" was always the response I received. Often, it was also, "I'm fine, stop asking." And better yet, sometimes it was just an eye roll or shitty look as a response with no words. I'm sure you have all gotten similar responses at some points in your lives.

Yes, this person was "fine" until the moment when they broke, resulting in an altercation at the office requiring police intervention. While the altercation happened after regular working hours, the impact was permanent. The negative stigma of mental health prevented this Gold Nugget from asking for help. And even though I wanted to be supportive, no resources, outlets, or programs were readily available. I saw the meltdown coming, but could do nothing to prevent it. Sure, we had an EAP (Employee Assistance Program), but for most employees this is just a brochure that HR gives you on your first day. Nothing more, and most certainly not something that was actually read by the employees.

Our EAP brochure, given out upon hire as part of our benefit programs and then subsequently during open enrollment annually, was not even close to a proactive or supportive solution, in my opinion. More programs, resources, and comfort yielding from belongingness should have been present in our workplace to be able to help support the Gold Nugget and possibly have avoided such a scene. No one was physically hurt, but quite honestly, it was embarrassing on all levels and resulted in both employees moving on to other opportunities.

The re-entry of respect into the workforce also positively impacts the mental health of both Gold Nuggets and Gold Bars. When you have happy, healthy pieces of gold, no matter the shape or size, they are relaxed, comfortable, and exhibit less stress. I know we all have examples of stressful working environments and how those made us feel. Those companies or organizations are lacking respect, and that negatively impacts the mental health of its employees regardless of Bar or Nugget status.

A CALL FOR CHANGE

So, what can we do about it?

How do we do better?

An example of outreach and one item that I did for all Gold Bars and Nuggets during the pandemic was to compile a list of mental health and similar resources for everyone and email it out periodically. This email included programs linked to insurance and our EAP, but it also included apps and similar programs that were free and easy to download and use on your phone with complete privacy. Also included were links to click on at home so they could take a virtual yoga or meditation class. We also included activities like local gyms or classes in nearby parks and community centers.

Now more than ever we need to focus on being proactive and helping to lay the groundwork for a happy and healthy workplace, which encompasses respect and understanding.

Mental health is merely a symptom, a burn from the volcanic activity. We are suffering from a lack of empathy and belonging. Our workplace demands have been counteracting our worth and wellbeing. We need to bring awareness to mental health care in the workplace and provide compassion to our Gold Bars and Nuggets who seek this. A judgment-free workplace and the proper resources to care for themselves are necessary for a happy, healthy, and productive work environment.

RESPECT

At the core of navigating this new landscape are common sense, respect, and treating others how you would want to be treated. Respecting that we are in a different working world now than we have ever been in, and also respecting where both our Gold Bars and Gold Nuggets are coming from. One is not right or proper over the other, but open communication, understanding, and general respect for each other can help pave the way for a bright, optimistic, and productive future where all feel understood and are genuinely happy with their working environments. This sense of happiness and belonging yields far more productive workers, positively impacting that bottom line regardless of what business or service you are part of.

CHAPTER SIX

RESPECT AND EMPATHY

My favorite definition of respect comes from the Oxford dictionary in which it is defined as "the due regard for the feelings, wishes, rights, or traditions of others." Please note, nowhere does it say that in order to respect something you need to also hold those same feelings, wishes, rights, or traditions, but a mere regard for them. These items that we speak of are formed over decades, and they are formed through our experiences, beliefs, the way we are raised, hardships, and even amazing triumphs.

Respect should be one of the easiest concepts and actions, yet we seem to have lost our way with it. I'm not suggesting that we are all the same, but we do need to respect and understand that each individual deserves the right to make their own decision and choices, whether you agree or not. You will never know all of the things another person is going through or has been through, and all of those experiences impact who they are, and who they will yet become. This is not your place to judge or critique, but instead to listen and respect. They have made their decisions and choices for specific reasons, and there is a good chance you will never know or understand them. Respect the areas where other human beings put their values, and know that it's more than okay to disagree and place your values elsewhere, but not to disrespect those choices. While the impetus of this book focuses on our workplaces, the messaging remains the same outside of those workplaces.

Respect in the workplace can take many forms, but one of the easiest is to just listen when someone else is speaking. Yeah, I know, intense stuff, right? Another form of respect in the workplace is being transparent. I think one of the largest lessons I have learned in my experiences is that when someone is harping on how transparent they are, this generally means they are hiding the biggest pile of shit ever. But let's say, for the sake of argument, this one is accurate, and we actually have a transparent relationship. And when I speak of transparency, I'm not suggesting that you tell your coworker about your deepest, darkest secrets, but instead a relationship where you level with someone, whether that is an easy or maybe more difficult discussion.

Walking one of your employees through their performance review is not always easy. Sometimes they are truly our Golden Nuggets and that review score is sky high, but there are also times when we have to counsel someone or possibly even put them on a Performance Improvement Plan. Being more direct with that information while still respecting them is key in addressing the issues at hand and trying to find a place to move forward from. Having and reporting factual information based on projects, hours, or similar is crucial in this space. There needs to be an understanding and a basis for this information so that you can now create a new and productive path for the future.

Being courteous and polite is yet another means of respect. Crazy, right? These are such basic fundamentals, but somehow we need a little reminder here and there on them.

Non-verbal body language is also a way of showing respect. Think about how you carry yourself or hold yourself when engaged in a conversation with someone else. We have all been in situations where you were trying to get a point across or explain something, and one of them who should be "listeners" on the other side is not even looking up but instead glued to their phone. While they can often repeat the last phrase or sentence you might have shared, a lot of times they are not able to go any deeper than that.

Additionally, I know we have all had times while either at work or home when you are engaged in a conversation and one of the recipients is sitting with arms folded and a scowl on their face. Maybe that has even been you at times. I know I am very much a participant in the "what the fuck is wrong with you" facial expression when I don't agree with something or someone. It takes effort to actively retract that initial tendency and focus on what is important and how to better address the issues or conversations that you may need to have. This does not mean that things will go your way. However, starting that conversation from a place of respect will generally yield a very different outcome, versus a pissy look on your face while asking what their problem is. And I can personally provide you this information from my past experiences and pissy faces.

Also, think about this in terms of cultural differences and the fact that certain body gestures mean one thing to one country or ethnicity, and something completely different elsewhere. One example of this is eye contact. In the U.S., we are crazy over this and constantly stare each other down in the eyes. However, in some cultures, such as Japan, constant eye contact like this is not friendly and instead is seen as rudeness and aggression. For those communicating internationally, this is huge, and knowing and researching these meanings are key for successful and respectful business partnerships, regardless of whether you are a Gold Bar or a Gold Nugget.

RESPECT FOR ALL

One of the biggest issues I have within the workplace is how people treat others, and this is not universal. It's worth mentioning here that folks are way more apt to be polite, courteous, respectful, and actively listening when it's a Gold Bar—but sadly, not as much so when they are interacting with a Gold Nugget. This is regardless of the level and position. And in my experience, it's generally the Gold Bars who are the worst offenders of this.

I had a Chief Operating Officer at a former company, and he was a brilliant example of this as he was a solid ass-kissing, polite douchebag when a fellow Gold Bar was around (especially those above him on the organizational chart) and would barely give anyone below him the time of day. Well, there *was* an exception to this. He would offer certain Gold Nuggets the time of day, but this was dependent on how tight their asses were and their relative bra cup size as well. I know we all know at least one of these. While the "Me Too" movement has created a different narrative around these cases and given many people a voice who had not previously had one, it certainly does not have the power to wipe the world clean of assholes.

From the start of my career, I have made it a point to treat everyone with respect and to treat everyone the same way, regardless of what your level, experience, or title is. I hold that respect through all of my meetings and interactions, regardless of what I might be feeling inside. My former General Counsel is a great example of a Gold Bar who does the same. At least within my presence and all interactions, he was very respectful to everyone he came in contact with, regardless of their Gold Bar or Gold Nugget level. This Gold Bar was also well aware of my affinity for four-letter words, specifically those beginning with the letter "f," but (and I am putting words in his mouth here) he also knew I took my job seriously and cared for the employees. He was a great example of a respectful Gold Bar making our workplace better by respecting us and allowing us to be our true selves.

I take you back to an interview where I was actually the interviewee to explain how impactful a lack of respect can be. I'm going to assume here that almost all of you can understand when I say that it's unreal how someone's words can replay in your mind and negatively impact your day, your week, and sometimes even longer. As I found myself sitting at my personal computer, wearing sweat shorts mixed with a tan blazer and navy blue tank, I was comfortable, ready, and willing to take part in a Zoom interview for a high-level HR position with a Biotech company in San Diego. The Gold Bar, or CEO, who I was meeting with had asked me to walk through my career and the choices I had made regarding the companies I had worked for. My initial thought…easy! I pour over a Cliffs' Notes version of my 20+ year career in HR with a primary focus on biotech, and as I end with my last company, I smile. Task completed, I think…or, you know, not.

It is at this point where the Gold Bar rubs his face with his hands for a good bit of time and says, "And without meaningful work for the past several months now?" I was taken aback, as earlier in my story I was completely clear on the fact that I had left my last employer (lovingly now coined as Satan's Circus) to be able to take care of personal matters, a.k.a. my dad being hospitalized and me instinctively feeling that I just needed to go home and see him. So yes, I was taken aback. I quickly responded with, "Excuse me?" And the Gold Bar just repeated the same question with the same exact wording.

To be clear with the timeline, I left Satan's Circus in March, and then went home for a couple of weeks to see my dad and family at the tail end of March, with my dad passing in April. I quickly flew back to the East Coast again for all of the arrangements and was back to the west side somewhere before the middle of May. This Zoom interview took place in very early June. In my mind I had not even had full processing time of everything that had taken place, and let's add to this the fact that during these tumultuous months, I had been surrounding myself with passion projects. I was working on writing a book, consulting in HR for clients who I truly loved, and still working as an adjunct professor for one of the nation's best educational institutions. So the dagger-sharp words of "without meaningful work" were just foreign to me. I still to this day have no idea how much time it takes to process and pick the pieces of your life back up, but I'm going to say less than three months all in wasn't too bad.

I was so caught off-guard that I replied simply, "I have been doing some consulting projects." His response: "Of course you have." Honestly, I'm not even sure what happened next in the interview, as my mental screen went blank for a few. I spent the rest of the day ruminating on the situation, and sadly that night sitting in the dark with tears in my eyes and two very wet sleeves from the prior ones that had already fallen that day. Was he right? Had I been so invested in my own pity party that I didn't see it? At the same time, I was so pissed and could not get past the words and utter lack of respect for my choices and what, in my mind, had been some of the worst months of my life. Respect and understanding are the cornerstone of any working, functioning relationship whether this is work, love, friendship, or anything else. I knew within an instant that I would never be able to work for this Gold Bar. I also knew that anyone who worked for this Gold Bar would never truly be respected, either.

THE BENEFITS OF RESPECT

Respect contributes to job satisfaction. This plays out for both the Gold Nugget who is satisfied and happy at work as well as the Gold Bar who is now also a happy employee yielding a steady workflow with no unexpected stoppages. Respect also creates a fair and unbiased work environment. Think about this for a minute and consider what it would be like to work for a company that held and respected Gold Bars and Gold Nuggets from all backgrounds, experiences, countries, etc. An unbiased, diverse workplace is one filled with respect where everyone is equal, regardless of their differences.

Respect also increases employee engagement. This means that both our Gold Nuggets and our Gold Bars are happy, productive, and present when working. Employee engagement is a direct reflection of work productivity. Nuggets and Bars who are happy and engaged are producing more, complaining less, and positively contributing to the bottom line. They have a vested stake and want to be part of the operation and directly contribute to it. This also yields increased collaboration. When Gold Bars and Nuggets are happy at work, that carries over into their teamwork, reaching across the line and going out of their way to assist another coworker and sometimes department with tasks needing to get done.

DIVERSITY, EQUITY, INCLUSION AND BELONGINGNESS

It goes without saying this diversification within your workforce produces positive, creative results that would not be achieved any other way. The concept of Diversity, Equity, Inclusion, and Belongingness (DEI&B) has become a cornerstone of today's workplace and certainly a topic that most are now familiar with, or have at least heard of at work or via training. However, without respect behind DEI&B, and true teeth within it, it holds no value to the company, nor will you see it positively impact performance or the organization's bottom line.

Countless studies explain the positive impact of DEI&B within an organization. Research heavy-hitters such as Deloitte, Harvard Business Review, and Forbes have all shown that diversity drives innovation—and innovation drives profitability. The more diverse an organization is, the more innovative and subsequently profitable they are. A diverse work population provides a cornucopia of options, including skills, education, opinions, and networks. Compare this with just one variety of fruit or vegetable on your Thanksgiving table. The bounty of the wealth is there in the cornucopia and provides for a feast of profitability. Within one of Deloitte's studies, they found that diverse workforces are twice as likely to meet or exceed their financial goals.[8] The proof is most definitely in the DEI&B data.

Sadly, the newest trend in this space is to retract these positions and "roll the function back into HR." Upon recent conversations with recruiters in the HR space, they "are up to their eyeballs" in DEI&B Nuggets and Bars, who they now need to find new positions. In a recent SHRM (Society for Human Resource Management) article, they highlight the trend of reducing these roles and, in some cases, eliminating them all together.[9] While major corporations generally begin these trends, it takes little to no time for them to carry through to organizations of all shapes and sizes. In this particular article, Amazon, Twitter, and Lyft were discussed, as they have already made drastic cuts in this area. In my opinion there are a few factors contributing to this new trend.

First, we have Gold Bars (as you've seen in my past) who believe they are "cured" as they have completed the scavenger hunt that is diversity and put a woman and/or other minority here or there throughout the company. Done! Or not even close; nor is this the intent of DEI&B.

Second, as I saw in my past, some Gold Bars believe DEI&B is achieved because they have completed a two-hour training and allowed for some of the working parents to leave in coordination with their child's school pick-up or drop-off. Or possibly held some aspect of an inclusive lunch or party for the holiday season. Again, we're not hitting the mark here.

Finally, I believe in large part there are various Gold Bars out there who do not truly respect the concept of diversity and don't see why or how they need to listen to some DEI&B touting person tell them what they should or should not do. A lot of times, the age-old belief that if it ain't broke, don't try and fix it comes in here. However, when you carry such biases with you, or don't even know about your biases, this is exactly what you would think because you just don't know any different.

Through respect we can encounter active listening and possible absorption of our biases and an approach to actually giving DEI&B the teeth it needs to do its job. Having a DEI&B Gold Bar in a position for one or even two years is not going to yield any impact to the bottom line without those teeth, and without having the respect of the Gold Bars and Nuggets to do the job they were hired to do.

EMPATHY

Empathy is another cornerstone I have spoken of thus far and is required by both Gold Nuggets and Bars to create a positive, productive, safe working environment. Empathy is the understanding of the feelings of another. Again, like respect, it's not a requirement that you have experienced the same situations, whether personal or through work. Nor does it mean that you agree with a person—it's a mere understanding of where they are coming from or what they may need to do their job, or possibly why they do it a certain way.

I believe a lot of Gold Bars only tend to have empathy for those going through situations they themselves have experienced. When we look at our Gold Nuggets, they are more apt to have empathy for everyone regardless of having gone through the same experience or not. This is largely due in part to the generational differences that exist generally between our Gold Bars and Gold Nuggets. This is also something I think our Gold Bars could certainly learn from and take from, as the Gold Nuggets have this one on lock.

One example from my time at Satan's Circus has to do with an employee who was mid-level, managing a team but not necessarily running a department. We're going to classify her as a Gold Nugget, but she's certainly close to that Bar status. Regardless, our Gold Nugget's mother was diagnosed with a late-stage illness and was requiring hospice. The other critical factor in this scenario is that our Gold Nugget's mother lived in China, so, as you know, immediately post-pandemic, this is not an easy trip to plan.

Our Gold Nugget applied for her visa with swift timing and was clear with the company that she needed to go to China. My response in these situations is always, "Please let us know what we can do to help. You need to take care of your family, and we will support you in whatever way possible." This is not necessarily the same viewpoint my Gold Bars held at Satan's Circus.

The quarantine requirements and restrictions were intense, and they were also ever-changing. Our local office Gold Bar was supportive of this and agreed to let the Gold Nugget work remotely, as much as possible, during her trip to China. As the weeks turned into months, sadly our Gold Nugget's mother passed away. The timing of her mother's passing was not ideal as it hit just around the holidays, and it had also happened near the end of her protected leave under the Family Medical Leave Act (FMLA). The Gold Nugget sent a message to both me and our local Gold Bar stating that her mother had passed and that she needed a few days but would be in touch once arrangements were made for her mom.

This is where our story takes an interesting turn, and why I'm using it as a lesson in empathy. As this situation was unfolding, so was the semi-monthly HR update meeting with all of us HR department Nuggets and Bars at Satan's Circus. Our leading Gold Bar quickly asks for a location update from my office and then questioned where exactly our Gold Nugget is, as her time has exhausted. I let them know that we were waiting to hear back from her on specifics of her return, but this was due to the fact that her mother just passed and she was making all of the arrangements. Let's also add to this the fact that the largest Chinese holiday was also going on, with most of the businesses shut down in celebration. With that, our Nugget's ability to get things done was required to halt for multiple days, as it was a time for family and not work. My Gold Bar's response: "This is a no call, no show." In HR terms, generally speaking, a "no call, no show" is when you have not heard from an employee, Nugget or Bar, for three days or shifts and so you are able to terminate.

As you might have already guessed, I was not quiet on this one. I quickly chimed in saying this was in no way, shape, or form a "no call, no show." Our Nugget's mother just passed, it was a national holiday, and we expected to be hearing from her in just a day or two as to the status of her leave and her planned return. My Gold Bar was not happy with this response and jumped right back on her "no call, no show" horse. I will admit, this meeting did not go great as I was a bit direct and honestly not willing to let them shovel this pile of shit onto our Nugget. The argument that I was having with my Gold Bar continued for a good bit of time in this meeting, as I was not letting this one go. In retrospect, I will apologize for my abrasiveness during this meeting, as it should have just been my Gold Bar and myself, but I do not apologize for my insistence and overall fighting for my Gold Nugget.

The meeting never cooled down, and I held my "heat" and "salt" over this situation for some time. The crazy part was that after this Zoom meeting ended, I had expected to see and hear support from my other HR team members. Instead, I received a call from one of my fellow HR Gold Nuggets who said that our Gold Bar was not wrong. I felt like I was working in an episode of *The Twilight Zone*, as I could not disagree more. Upon hearing this, I was even more heated on the topic. Our Gold Nugget's mother just died. Our Nugget was in a different country, alone, and was caring for her mother with very little outside support. In China, you are responsible for your elders. The care systems we are accustomed to in the U.S. are not the same that we see in other countries. Specifically, in this case, tradition and culture dictate that family is responsible for aging elders.

Up until this point immediately following the passing of her mother, our Gold Nugget had been in communication the entire time, not dropping the ball, not letting her team down, and never avoiding or unnecessarily passing off work onto others while dealing with her family situation. The entire time, our Nugget had been transparent and present regardless of the time difference and situations being dealt with on the other side of the globe. I will also add that our Gold Nugget attended virtual meetings, even though it was 3 a.m. in her time zone.

HOW COULD THEY BE SO CRUEL?

So, what was the reasoning from both my Gold Bar and fellow colleague, Gold Nugget? In both cases and in different conversations, they stated they did not go through this when their mothers passed away.

Empathy is about listening, and it is also about understanding where someone is at or why they might need or request an accommodation. Empathy does not mean you dealt with the same situation the same way. Nor does empathy place an emotional barometer on a situation, saying you should feel X or Y but not Z. At the end of the day, I do not give one flying shit how you did or did not deal with the death of a parent. That was never in question here.

At this time and space, it was about understanding where our Gold Nugget was and what her possible limitations might be. It was about respecting her and providing her the leverage to take care of her life and family needs, while still managing the work aspects she had agreed to take care of while abroad. If there had been a break in communication, work productivity, or availability while she was gone, that would be a very different situation. But we did not experience that, and she was communicative and present the entire time leading up to the passing of her mother.

It's still surreal to talk about this situation and relive it by writing it down. To this day, I am still in awe of how this situation played out. I had expected this to be a no-brainer and come to a consensus that would benefit both the organization and the Gold Nugget. In the HR world, I would never sacrifice business necessity as that is what pays the bills, and our paychecks, but in this case our Gold Nugget was nothing but proactive with communication every step of the way through this journey. That one exception was the few days just following the passing of her mother, but even still, we had the email to both our local Gold Bar and myself. In my opinion there was never a dropped ball by our Gold Nugget anywhere along this path, and Satan's Circus should have been more understanding, as there was no direct impact on the Nugget's team, the company, or the productivity that could not otherwise be handled for those few days. As a side note, our Gold Nugget never even knew any of this had transpired in her absence.

It goes without saying that this played a huge factor in my decision when I left Satan's Circus. My dad had fallen at the end of January, and the prior example had just happened the preceding holiday season. The doctors were not providing reasonable answers on my dad's condition and his health, and while being at the hospital, he was rapidly declining at an alarming rate. Needless to say, with that experience and the knowledge of how difficult they were to deal with through this, I knew that my internal feelings of needing to go home and see my dad would never be understood. Just because you did or did not have the same or similar experience does not negate the situation, feelings, or personal needs that a Gold Bar or Nugget may have.

This experience was the last straw for me. I was hell-bent on my feelings of needing to go home, and I knew that these ass clowns would not support the time that I felt I needed, so quitting was my only option. To their credit, my Gold Bar did remind me I had a few days of vacation that I could use for the trip. Okay, sure.

As you may have guessed, I did quit my job and went home to see my family rather swiftly. It was only three days after that two-week trip home when my father passed. I would not have traded that trip home and seeing him alive for anything in the world. And I would never, in a million fucking years, have ever forgiven myself if I did not listen to my internal voice and take that time to see him. While I am saddened by this example of lack of empathy and understanding, I am forever grateful for it, as this was the kick in the ass I needed to walk out of the circus tent.

WE NEED UNDERSTANDING

With both respect and empathy come understanding. When you respect someone's place or ideas, you are not necessarily in agreement, but instead in a place of understanding. You do not need to agree; you just need to listen and have an open mind to a thought process that may be different from yours. With empathy, again, you are listening and being present with someone else's narrative, regardless of your agreeance on or with it. As a natural byproduct of both respect and empathy, you create a safe and understanding space, hence the link between concepts. I would say at this point I've likely had thousands of Gold Bars and Nuggets walking through my door just to be heard and understood, just needing a place to release all of the thoughts circling their brains.

You can see this through my examples as well as those you have lived through or witnessed yourself. This is a critical component that costs absolutely nothing to implement but provides immense returns with productivity of a company's Gold Bars and Gold Nuggets. Understanding simply means you are listening and comprehending something. I know this has been mentioned several times already, but understanding does not mean you have to agree or that you have the same experiences or feelings. It simply means you can grasp where this Gold Nugget or Gold Bar is coming from. There is no right or wrong, but instead an awareness that yields an immense amount of relief for the impacted Nugget or Bar.

The weight that this understanding lifts is almost immeasurable. I think back to an experience at a prior biotech about four years prior to my dad's passing. My dad had been at work on a Friday and was whisked off in an ambulance on Sunday. We won't dive into the nitty-gritty except to say that his medical condition was largely unknown. The doctors were taken aback and did not have a diagnosis or direction when he was first admitted to the hospital. At this time in my career, I had just started a brand-new job. *Of course*, you say! These challenges in life tend to find us at our most vulnerable times with little to no "extra time" or space in our calendars.

My new job was about one week old when this happened. My family is not the most medically inclined, but with my career and experiences in a similar space, I needed to know what was going on. This was a lot of time on the phone with his doctors back East, and even more so via the game of phone tag that I would play with them prior to connecting. Regardless of that fun, I tell you this to share an amazing example of caring and compassion.

One of my Gold Bars at the new company, an MD, called me to ask how he could help and told me to forward my dad's medical charts over to him for review and insight. Let's add to this the fact that my CEO, the Goldest of Bars at the company, also offered to lend a hand. He pulled me aside to tell me whatever I needed, whether that was going home, taking calls, or his medical opinion…it was mine, and all I needed to do was say the word.

I need to specify here that I was not soliciting their help or input. I *did* inform our admin so that someone knew where I was if I was on a phone call or similar, but I did not take it beyond that within our organization. Starting a new job is always scary, and I certainly did not want to rock any boats. This was no Satan's Circus, folks, and I cannot express how much this meant coming from these Bars who had known me only one or two weeks. Think about the differences between this story versus the others and the impact on my situation, my mental health, and my overall well-being.

What this meant was that when I did go home (and it was only for a few days), I was working the entire time. I worked on the flights, escaped the hospital here and there for calls, and did 1,000% of whatever I could to not let them down the way they had not let me down with simple respect and empathy. They may not have handled my situation the same if they had been in my shoes, but that didn't matter, and I never once heard those words. It was an act of respect and understanding of what I needed at that time. That respect and understanding were paid back to them in spades by the engagement and effort I now dedicated to their visions and needs. The reciprocal relationship is beneficial on all sides, and the gratitude lasts long beyond the time in life we are dealing with those challenges.

EMPATHY AND RESPECT HAVE A HUGE ROI

Interestingly, *Harvard Business Review* magazine[10] published an article on a study done by Georgetown University's Christine Porath regarding respect in the workplace in which both Bars and Nuggets were asked if they felt respected in their organizations. Within the study, almost 20,000 employees spanning the globe were surveyed. What they found was that when asked what mattered most to the workers, it was respect from their supervisors, or Gold Bars. Yet, the trends in a lot of our organizations point in the opposite direction with more and more disrespectful behavior being reported.

A key takeaway from this study is that a workplace exhibiting respect yields higher productivity and employee engagement. This is a result of those employees being satisfied at work and, in turn, staying loyal to those companies. They are more resilient and show higher performance in both creativity and taking direction from their Gold Bars. The flip side of the research shows that 80% of employees experiencing disrespectful treatment spent significant work time ruminating on that behavior versus performing their assigned tasks. To add to this, of those Bars and Nuggets ruminating on disrespectfulness, 48% of them deliberately reduced their work efforts.

In summary, a workplace short on respect and empathy will also be short on productivity. A workplace that is blooming in respectful flowers will also be blooming in increased productivity and overall happy, loyal Bars and Nuggets.

CHAPTER SEVEN

THE HOW-TO GUIDE

This is the part of the book where we flip the script. This is where you can take all the things I have mentioned thus far and turn them into actionable items for you and your workplace, or life in general. By incorporating these small, cost-free steps into your regular routines, you can create a sustainable change within your working relationships and your organization. Within leadership styles and theory, this is called relational leadership. Relational leadership relies on small, frequent interactions with your coworkers that, over time, create a lasting and steadfast foundation for relationships. These frequent but fundamental factors lead to a workplace of respect and understanding where both our Gold Bars and

Gold Nuggets are happy to come to work and yield increased productivity as a result of those environmental factors.

LISTENING

We start our "How-to Guide" with listening. It sounds too easy, right? There are actually a lot of moving parts when it comes to active listening. Throughout my career, I would say that the majority of the people who stop by my office just want to be heard. At least 60% of them start the conversation by asking, "Do you have a minute?" or can they "ask me a quick question?" Side note: these are huge pet peeves with me as you technically already asked me a "quick question," and in my experience a "quick question" doesn't exist. I digress…within my experience, over half of the folks who walk into my office just want to be heard. They are not asking for things, they are not reporting things; they simply want a space to unload and/or feel heard.

Feeling and knowing they are valued for their contributions and being treated with respect (you know, like an adult) is something that should be done automatically. That is key here. Again, these are all free things to organizations. So then why is it so hard to practice? In part, I believe the answer to this question lies in the unrealistic and growing pile of shit we need to do or take care of. We are all constantly multitasking in one way, shape, or form, and to be a good Gold Bar or even fellow-supporting Gold Nugget, we need to put the phone down, remove our eyes from the screen in front of us, and be present with the folks around us.

I believe this is something we all need to be aware of, Nugget or Bar, and remind ourselves of. I know myself there have been a bunch of times when I was under a tight deadline and needed to get something done when a "quick question" walked into my door. I would never lie to you and tell you that I was always present and listening. I can be a solid asshole when the moment presents itself, but most times I caught myself in this practice and put the phone down or purposefully turned my monitor off. I know, some of you are shuttering now.

This is one area where both Bars and Nuggets need to improve. All of us, throughout all of the generations, have become horrible listeners. I know just from speaking with some of my cousins and younger Nuggets, they don't even look up when talking to me. Just take a look around the restaurant the next time you are out to dinner. How many tables are filled with families all sitting on their phones, yet having some sort of non-engaging conversation? Put the tech down, people—this is not going to fix itself.

We should be practicing this everywhere…in the workplace, at school, and most importantly with our families and friends. No time is ever a guarantee, and these moments are precious. Coming from the workplace specifically, this is critical. Know your audience and know where you are. I have had countless times when I was leading a New Hire Orientation class and could not get my attendees' full attention. I'm sure you can assess how incredibly shy I am, so I'm not afraid to call these Nuggets and Bars out. I expect their attention, regardless of level or position.

A huge part of listening is also shown through your body language. You don't need to be physically speaking—it's shown in the way you carry yourself, in the gestures you make, and in the eye contact or lack thereof. I like to suggest the approach that you would listen to someone else the way you would expect to be listened to if it were you. How would you want to be treated? Then act accordingly. This is easy so long as you exhibit a little bit of effort, and that effort goes a long way as respect for your coworkers, whether they are Nuggets or Bars.

To take this a step further, when we listen emphatically, we are creating a comfortable space for discussion and providing our audience with a map to guide the conversation. This is not about how you experienced something or dealt with something. Instead, this is about listening and acknowledging their feelings. You are being compassionate and understanding, withholding judgment. Again, there is no right or wrong in these cases, nor is it about your agreeance or your disagreeance. It is about being present and allowing them the safe space they need.

Providing this safe space builds a great foundational relationship filled with trust and understanding. This also yields an increase in productivity of both Bars and

Nuggets alike. We also have to address the impact this has on collaboration and problem-solving. When you face challenges at work, often you are doing so with a team, and this enables that team to work together more successfully. When Nuggets and Bars feel more comfortable and trust their working space and environment, they are more apt to share ideas and suggestions. When they feel put down or not respected, they will not share that information and instead sit quietly until the meeting is over. The positive and collaborative environment created by a workplace filled with respect and empathy is critical in a progressive, positive, and productive workplace.

RECIPROCAL MENTORSHIP

Mentorship is when guidance is provided by a peer— typically someone more experienced—and exists for both Bars and Nuggets. This is the general way we see mentorship, and it certainly can be an amazingly positive and educational path for whoever is on it. But for our purposes, I want to focus on reciprocal mentorship. This is when both parties are learning from each other, versus a more experienced Gold Bar mentoring a Gold Nugget in the traditional sense.

Exchanging information and learning from each other is far more beneficial and should be part of all of our workplaces. There is no one omniscient person, whether a Gold Bar or a Gold Nugget, who knows everything, and nor should we want to live in and be part of an environment where that was the case.

Let's think for a minute about the more common approach to mentorship and the benefits that could be gained from it. If we use reciprocal mentoring from the standpoint of inclusion, we can expand our world immensely into areas we have not previously experienced. Reciprocal mentorship offers a sharing space where all are created equal and everyone has a voice. This is about exploring and understanding one another to bring a powerful yet human relationship element into the workspace.

The power behind this concept is expansive, as it provides a space for a Gold Nugget to share and express how they feel, and what it's like to work for this employer. This offers a completely different mindset and opinion from that of the other Gold Bars. When was the last time you felt heard or understood by one of your leaders? Think back to a prior work gathering or holiday party, and where were your Gold Bars? At least in my experience, we generally had all of the middle-aged, white, male Gold Bars hanging out in one corner, and the rest of us, not fitting within the aforementioned parameters, were off on the other side of the party. This is a visual exploration, but one I'm sure almost all of us have seen. What if it didn't have to be that way? We need to look for places and spaces where we can merge these two worlds into one.

Reciprocal mentorship would offer a step in that direction, providing power and cohesiveness from a place of diversity and mixing things up a bit. One item worth mentioning is that a safe space is an absolute must with this type of program or else it will not work. If our Nuggets and Bars do not feel safe, they will not be open to sharing and will likely clam up, or say that everything is fine when it's not. I know I have certainly done so a time or two in my past, and I'm sure you can think of places where you did as well. Let's now compare this to an environment where all voices have power and are encouraged to speak up. The lessons and discussions being learned from those open and free workspaces are priceless and in some cases lead to change—dynamic, inclusive change.

Mentorship, whether we are exploring standard or reciprocal, is an amazing leadership development tool with great success. This is often present in company cultures that support and foster educational and growth opportunities. I worked for a non-profit for a bit of time, and they were hands-down brilliant with the concept of mentorship. The general practice was for the manager or Gold Bar to send the mentor with the new employee or mentee, but I preferred to take it one step further. When we had Gold Nuggets interested in an area where we focused, I would set them up with one of those mentors.

We had an amazingly smart new hire who was straight out of a biotech program at a top school in Southern California. He had taken a job that was primarily customer service but did so with the thought of gaining some industry experience, and then the long-range plan was an application to law school. By taking the LSAT myself, I knew this Gold Nugget was most definitely going to law school. He was way smarter than me and much more focused. Don't get me wrong, I can throw down if I want to, but we're painting with broad strokes here.

His intent with law school was well known, and so my focus was a mentor who was in our legal group, lobbying and working in Washington, DC. Now, the hiring Gold Bar was not within legal and instead in customer service—sales to be exact. So, I'm sure you can now see that the Gold Bar was not a fan of my selection, as she felt the newly hired Gold Nugget should forever be in this customer service role. In the end, I had to wave my white flag and yield to the hiring manager's wishes, but I will also tell you that I set up a legal mentorship anyway, on the side.

When Gold Bars and Nuggets are engaged and interested, they are so much more present and happy within their workspace and environment. His goal was law school, and I had absolutely no doubt that he would end up there and I truly wanted to support that endeavor. We do not hire folks to work for a lifetime anymore like we had seen in past generations. I know from my experience, and you may recall from your own, it was my grandfather who worked at Bethlehem Steel for over fifty years. This does not exist anymore. In comparison, we know the younger generations are moving on, and rather swiftly, even as they start the job.

So, why would we not make them happy for the time we have them and yield astronomically higher productivity for that period of time?

I often explain this via lessons learned from my students. In addition to my day job, I have been teaching college courses adjunctly for several years now and also have a course published online that students can take for free. In my classes I require a couple of presentations, as this is important in our profession because we are often speaking in front of people. So one of these presentations is on HR law. Please put yourself in my shoes here, as a class filled with awkward student presentations on HR law feels like an eternity. They hate speaking in front of others, they generally hate law, and now we are adding an application of HR to that. Trifecta for "please fucking kill me now," which has on occasion been written in my grading notebooks while they are talking.

Let's compare this with presentations they later give in the semester on the fictitious company they have created for class and are now fictitiously hiring for. I do not tell them what kind of company to create—what I do encourage is that it's a place of passion. When I tell you that these presentations are absolutely and astronomically more engaged, active, pleasant, and informative, it's still an under exaggeration. I cannot even give you the words to describe the overall differences in these students when allowed to cover a passion project versus U. S. laws in HR. This is the exact same as my mentorship example above. In that example, the "U.S. laws in HR" is our customer service mentor, while the passion project is our law mentor. Which one do you think worked best and yielded a more positive result for the entire company? It's clearly the law mentorship.

When we engage in such a way, we not only foster and yield benefits from being present, but we also tend to see that Gold Bar or Nugget remains with our organization for a longer period of time. When employees, regardless of Bars or Nuggets, are engaged, and feeling respected and heard, they are much less likely to leave our organization and will yield higher productivity than their counterparts.

With the reciprocal mentor programs, we have an even and free flow of information both ways. This enables our Gold Bars to learn from our Gold Nuggets, and vice versa. Not any one of us knows everything, and taking a step back to provide a clear runway for this information exchange will benefit the entire organization by providing a diverse successful team and an increase in workplace productivity.

DEI&B

Within our "How-to Guide" we need to revisit Diversity, Equity, Inclusion, and Belonging (DEI&B) as respect cannot be addressed without these factors. DEI&B is at the forefront of employment right now regardless of your level, field, or industry. This area has evolved rapidly over the past few years. As a society, we have seen this evolution as a result of systemic racism, social injustice, and inequality. Overall, this movement conveys a message to employers, and certainly our Gold Bars, of the need to be more understanding and more empathetic.

Generally speaking, diversity came first. Diversity was primarily thought of in terms of having a team of Bars and Nuggets from varying backgrounds and ethnicities. But that did not necessarily mean those Bars and Nuggets felt welcomed or valued. Nor did it mean their input was going to be heard or listened to, so diversity alone was not enough to solve the problem.

Within our workplaces, at least in my experience, diversity and inclusion were lumped together. If you were to ask a Gold Bar or Nugget working outside of HR, they would likely tell you they were both the same thing—hiring people from different places. While maybe we have a piece of it, we are missing a bit more. For inclusion, it is more about celebrating those differences through unique ideas, experiences, and backgrounds. Inclusion creates a feeling of belonging where those differences are positively highlighted and benefit the team overall.

Equity's addition is to ensure that all Gold Bars and Gold Nuggets have access to the same opportunities, regardless of what differences may or may not exist. Some Bars and Nuggets would say this is about women being provided fair pay for their jobs, and while this is brilliantly accurate, it does not cover the entire concept. This is also about providing opportunities to everyone regardless of differences like gender, sexual identification, financial background, etc. It is truly providing equal compensation and equal opportunity regardless of who you are or where you come from.

Belonging is really the key to bringing all of these pieces together. This is where you feel comfortable and safe and are respected for who you are, as you are. Belongingness provides all workers, Bars and Nuggets alike, with a safe space where they can be who they truly are and not be afraid to express their ideas, suggestions, and thoughts regardless of the scenario. This creates strengthened relationships where everyone communicates to solve problems, work collaboratively, and exist in a happy, healthy working environment.

DEI&B is an immense powerhouse within respect and empathy and can drive company culture to a positive and productive place. This, however, is not achieved by one training a year. Nor is this achieved by a leadership team composed of Gold Bars who do not actually believe in it. Instead, these are practices that must encompass walking the walk and talking the talk.

My favorite part of being the interviewee is actually asking my questions. One of my top questions asked every single time is for them to describe the company culture in their own words and their experiences. Many times diversity tops that list, but when I dig down to ask what or how the company exhibits that to them, on several occasions I've had the following answer: "We did a training last year on it." This does not exemplify having a diverse culture. Because you have one woman or one black man on your Gold Bar leadership team does not make a diverse team. I smile knowing inside that if I were to take a job with a company like that, I would need to do a lot of work and a lot of education.

Do not get me wrong, offering or mandating a class on diversity in your workplace is an amazing place to start. However, this is not the pinnacle of the mountain. Instead, this is the initial pawn on "Go" on our Monopoly board of working life. We are just starting and have not even moved around the board yet, or gotten to "Free Parking" for that matter. While our training may be our starting point, ensuring that our Gold Bars and Nuggets are actually living these values and reflecting them in the day-to-day activities is key.

We all know that actions speak louder than words, and this concept is a case in point. We want to see actions—changes within the recruitment and hiring process that ensure diversity and equity. For example, having an interview team, providing them with evaluation metrics, and ensuring that each candidate is treated the same is one way to secure a healthy interview process. Compiling a DEI&B team of Gold Bars and Gold Nuggets from varying departments, backgrounds, and levels within the organization is another way to support and live DEI&B. Other ways to measure and impact DEI&B would be: retention levels, pay equity, employee satisfaction, and resource allocation. Addressing the fact that personal responsibility is held by all Bars and

Nuggets is critical in creating a company culture supportive of and including DEI&B. Additionally, providing your Bars and Nuggets with the tools, information, and ability to point out areas needing corrections is also paramount.

Managing this process is continuous, and buy-in from all levels is crucial to the success of these values. This is fully about respecting and understanding that everyone is different, and this is not only okay but amazing as it provides productivity, worker happiness, and overall job satisfaction for Gold Nuggets and Bars alike. These practices must be nurtured and celebrated for all that they bring to the organization.

For some organizations this can be an immense hill to climb. I respect that as well, but our leaders must be willing. Throughout my career I have been lucky enough to work with some of the best speakers and most knowledgeable Gold Bars I've ever met in this space. One particular Gold Bar is a black male with a PhD who has been thrown into so many hostile situations it's unreal, but he always keeps his cool and uses the examples as lessons for his future students. Some of the best advice ever given to me by this Gold Bar was that as HR, I was not able to move a boulder like DEI&B up the hill by myself. These "boulders" had to start at the top and roll down.

Sadly, the company where I worked at that time was not in a place where the mountain peak was a believer in DEI&B. Was it an initiative on the corporate goals? Yes. Was this touted as part of the culture? Yes. Was the walk being walked and the talk being talked? Not even close. I scheduled a training for our executive Gold Bars about unconscious bias. The training was amazing and engaging and provided so much foundational knowledge to set the team off on the right path. Despite this, afterward I found myself listening to two Gold Bars who attended the session say how it was bullshit and not applicable in their workplace.

This is just simply not true. While I'm in no way, shape, or form some sort of HR vigilante, I was absolutely heartbroken since this should be a fundamental block in the structure of the organization. I did try a couple of other ways to approach the issue, but the preferred method was to throw money at it and donate to something of a diverse cause. While donations are certainly a form of support, they will not change the corporate culture, nor will they change how Nuggets and Bars feel about working for a company that cannot be bothered with such "trivial bullshit." Instead, here is $20.

What this example signifies is an utter lack of respect and empathy. Within this example there is only one way, and that is the Gold Bar way. This is not an environment I want to be part of. This is not to say that you can't make mistakes, or retool or edit the way you are running a program such as your interview structure so that it's fair and unbiased. That is amazing and we all need to edit from time to time, but this was an utter disregard for anyone outside of their special Gold Bar bubble and so blatant that they did not even mind saying it in front of me and in one case, to me.

The diversification of a team and addition of DEI&B benefits the company immensely. The data comes from all avenues and studies, but the same takeaway exists within all of the reports: DEI&B strengths the company providing a competitive advantage with better problem solving skills, productivity, and employee engagement. This is the result of a diverse team that is treated fairly and feels comfortable and safe in their environment to work together for the best interest of the company.

Within one study conducted by Deloitte[11], they found that DEI&B offers a company an increase of 46% of a competitive advantage with the industry, and 40% found with more accurate decision-making skills. An additional study[12] shows that organizations with strong DEI&B cultures were two times more likely to meet their business goals, and also indicated that 72% were more innovative as compared with companies lacking in a DEI&B culture. The proof is certainly in the numbers.

VOLUNTEERISM

As we explore respect and empathy, I have to take us to my favorite location on this journey: volunteerism. In my industry we are a bit spoiled. These are tough jobs with high risk but also high reward, and sometimes we forget just how good we have it when compared to those who are working their literal asses off in manual labor, as well as those who are suffering in our communities. Overall, I have been immensely lucky in my career and worked with some super awesome Gold Bars and Gold Nuggets. Within all of those experiences, the one place we were all truly able to come together as one was by giving back within our community. The benefits of volunteerism are lasting and stay with our Gold Bars and Gold Nuggets far beyond the four-hour shift we have at the food bank or such. They not only help our communities, but they help our teams and our working relationships.

The best way I can explain this is by likening it to an old tile floor or countertop. We know over time that grout begins to erode or fade, and sometimes we're even missing entire pieces of it. In this case, those tiles are our Gold Bars and Gold Nuggets who are being regrouted by our volunteerism. The volunteerism, time, and action are the grout. The experience of working together for a greater good and cause fills in those gaps and crevasses naturally and without any force.

Personally speaking, philanthropies were something I was familiar with since way back in my collegiate Sister Spirit days. It's okay, you can laugh. I still laugh at those experiences, but the memories I love, the ones I have taken with me for well over twenty years, are the ones where we were serving our community. With working in HR, I often seek these opportunities out without initially considering the future outcome and lasting positive impact on our employees. My focus is not initially on the Gold Bars and Nuggets, but instead on the food banks, with homeless and pet shelters, with the fundamental supplies and labor to feed and nurture our local communities. And when exploring these opportunities, let's not just focus on Thanksgiving, folks—these organizations and philanthropies are always in need.

A great example of this comes from my experience in working for a non-profit organization. Serving the community was part of what we did as a job, but in a very specific sector and not necessarily outside of that. I set up an event as a way to have all Bars and Nuggets work together and bridge some gaps we were experiencing generationally. Within this organization we had some Gold Bars who were with the organization for a long time, say more than seven years. Then we added a new wave of Gold Nuggets who were much younger and with the organization maybe eighteen months or less. Needless to say, we had some gaps to bridge. That was the true intent of the activity. While that was certainly a result of our efforts, that was not the only result we experienced.

Fridays historically were a joke in the office, with little to no work being accomplished unless you had a project deadline you were trying to meet. This was part of our company culture. Most of the staff worked from home on Fridays, so the twelve of us who actually came in were not necessarily excited about it and didn't always put in 110%, if you know what I mean. I would say maybe 40% of actual work was getting accomplished on Fridays in our office, so when I set this activity, I did so on a Friday as we were not missing too much. I had signed us up for a volunteer date at a local food bank. As we got to the food bank for our shift, we all signed our waivers and sat for our educational session on safety. The volunteer coordinators explained the jobs available for our shift and gave an overall informative session about who the food bank served and how. Our Bars and Nuggets were able to select the duties they wanted such as checking expiration dates, can or food packaging imperfections, packing, sorting—just lots of options, as they needed the help across the board.

Toward the end of our shift, we had some different options for things to do like clean-up and a side project for the weekend. The side project is where our story gets interesting. As you may recall, this was a Friday. At this food bank on Fridays, they build weekend kits for the children who are in school and do not have food at home to eat over the weekends. School is what provides some of our community children with a steady, warm meal. Those on this project packaged the following for each child: seven tangerines or oranges, two cans of soup, one can of tuna, and one small box of dry cereal.

What happened that day was that our entire staff, Gold Bars and Nuggets, received a lesson in how amazingly lucky we are, and also how much help our community needs. This weekend kit is what our local underserved students are getting to take home so they have food until school starts again on Monday. While I'm generally dead inside, emotionally speaking, I was taken aback. But what I grossly underestimated was how this had impacted our volunteering Gold Bars and Nuggets.

There were tears in our office later that afternoon, and when I asked what was wrong or what happened, I was surprised by the answer. It was about the food bags for the kids so they would have things to eat during the weekend. I'm HR. When I see tears, it's usually about someone getting hurt either at work or possibly about issues in their personal lives. I most certainly did not expect it to be tears for our community. I did not expect this event to have such a profound impact on our employees.

Weeks later, in an all-staff meeting someone presented pictures from our volunteer event, as we did have a few folks who were not able to make it. After that short presentation, we had more discussion and even more tears from our Gold Bars and Nuggets on this very topic. This was such a strong ass bridge that had been built across these varying levels of experience and generations that I could never have imagined something so powerful, and now indestructible, being built through one philanthropic shift. To this day, I get emotional when sharing this story. I have never been more proud of my colleagues, and I don't believe this experience will ever be forgotten by any of us who shared in it.

This exercise was about finding common ground and building something together while utilizing everyone's strengths, regardless of what those were or what job they chose to do. All of the jobs, all of the individuals, were so critically important in coming together through respect, empathy, and understanding in completing that one shift on one random Friday. Imagine what would be possible if you could harness energy such as that for your company, or even department? Imagine what goals could be accomplished and what problems could be solved. It's these cornerstone foundations that create happiness, belonging, and positive contributions within your employees and foster productivity.

For what it's worth, even months later, those relationships and generational differences were forever changed. They worked together more across varying departments, they actually looked forward to it, and they had more fun at work. Employee engagement was increased, as was productivity and that ever-illusive statement of a smile on my Gold Bars' and Nuggets' faces. Imagine that.

Volunteerism also provides a great space to solicit your Gold Bars' and Nuggets' input on what philanthropic events or organizations they would like to support. It's easy and fun to be able to switch it up and change that focus from time to time. Within my experience, there is generally one organization supported by the company, and then sometimes we do a survey or similar to see what other charities and events the Gold Bars and Nuggets are interested in to be able to add to our mix. As we are dealing with post-pandemic times and restrictions, some of these may not be available in the way they once were, but I assure the opportunity to give back and support your local community very much exists. This not only supports your community but your Gold Bars, Nuggets, team work, and even productivity. *Harvard*

Business Review reports that volunteerism activities increase employee engagement and drastically impact our Gold Bars' and Nuggets' overall happiness and employee satisfaction.[13]

CHAPTER EIGHT

A CASE STUDY

In this Case Study we are going to compare a successful and respectful leadership style with that of an unsuccessful and disrespectful leadership style. The paradox of belonging and/ or identity is the focus of this case study. As we examine this paradox, we do so in the face of an organization rebranding and large staff reduction due to a new CEO's leadership. Within the belonging paradox we focus on the beliefs and values of belonging to an organization compared with a newly branded version of that organization encompassing different values, beliefs, and workplace culture. The intent of this section is to show you my real-life experiences with an overall positive working environment as compared with one that was, in my opinion, toxic.

SCENARIO ONE

In the first case, our biotech organization was facing challenging times. With a depleting stock price, our Board of Directors and Head Gold Bar, who was our CEO and one of the founding members of the company, made an announcement that he would be resigning. This was a swift decision made effective immediately, resulting in our company having a temporary CEO Gold Bar put in place. The temporary leader was one of our Board Members. He was not a fan favorite of any of the employees, but everyone knew this would be short-lived, and we had high hopes for the new CEO Gold Bar to be hired.

At this point in time, we had over 200 employees, and what they did not know was that behind the scenes we were having a difficult time finding a new CEO Gold Bar willing to take the reins of what could be considered a sinking ship. It was approximately four or five months before we found a new CEO Gold Bar, who happened to be the third option out of three possibilities. The others had been made offers but declined, even with salary and package negotiations.

The new Gold Bar's past was that of a slicing and dicing mentality seen with previous biotech companies that he ran and eventually closed. Despite the understanding that layoffs were inevitable, there was still a sense of hope that we would work through this difficult transition.

Our company culture and values were evident in everything we did and how we did them. Our entire company felt a sense of belonging, and this company was a huge part of our identity and pride for Gold Bars and Gold Nuggets alike. And while we didn't always agree, we were all respected and understood. Nothing is ever perfect, but that respect and overall passion for our organization was what had gotten us through so many roller coaster rides in the past. The beliefs and values that we held so dear, like loyalty, respect, integrity, and innovation, were part of our company culture and ingrained in all of us.

Our Gold Nuggets and Gold Bars were loyal employees, as our attrition prior to this was almost non-existent. At one point we were just under 500 employees, but in our industry we tend to see lots of ebbs and flows, with swift hiring and large reductions as well. Even after layoffs, as we could hire employees back, we would most often start by bringing back our former Gold Nuggets and Gold Bars.

As head of HR for the organization, I was front and center in what we labeled as "right-sizing." Per executive meetings with our leaders, I learned that we would go from 200 employees to thirty-four, and this included the twelve or so people who were in the room at the time. There were no discussions, no questions, no respect, as this was the way it was—end of story. It's a paradox in and of itself to be working in that situation knowing that your friends and colleagues are mostly gone, but that you have a job to do whether you like or agree with your Gold Bar or not.

The timing was supposed to have been at least three months to give us the opportunity to prepare all the termination documents, create contingency plans for the six buildings we had on our campus, and get our ducks in a row. Instead, we were given a new mandate that the "right-sizing" would happen in three weeks.

The employees who remained were the best and brightest, for sure. They were also very much part of our strong company values, beliefs, and culture. However, the damage of the massive layoffs and our new leader had been done. Despite being selected to stay, we had two Gold Nuggets walk right out and would not even discuss staying with us. They respected themselves too much and quit on the spot, wanting no part of what was already being coined as the "new regime."

The weeks that followed were even more difficult for the Gold Nuggets and Gold Bars who remained. There was no sense of belonging, and our identities had been stripped. I tried to focus my attention on those employees, but I also had a new directive to help build up the new branding via staffing. It was not even two weeks after the reductions that I was tasked with recruiting five new people and doing so right away. Our prior culture was heavily focused on clinical research and scientific staff, while the new rebranding of our company was more focused on project management.

Despite the news and what was happening with our company, I was able to fill the positions and do so rather quickly. The used car salesmanship that our new CEO Gold Bar had was remarkable, and he sold these new beliefs and values brilliantly to the oncoming staff. With such a small organization, he was able to interact with everyone but made it very clear that he did not want any ideals, beliefs, or old ways of doing things to be present. It was a very different company now—it was quicker, sleeker, and focused on his brand of business versus the science that was our primary focus in the past.

The new CEO Gold Bar quickly befriended the new hires and also brought on some of his past Gold Bars to help him run the organization. It was very easy to walk down a hallway and be able to see who was part of the "old tapestry" and who was part of the "new regime." Work performance was almost non-existent for the legacy Gold Bars and Gold Nuggets, while the newly hired Gold Bars and Gold Nuggets were running on all cylinders. With most of the executives being new as well, the newly hired Gold Nuggets and Bars all formed bonds together rather quickly, almost avoiding the legacy employees in entirety.

I did ask for our new CEO Gold Bar's assistance in working with both sides, the new hires and the legacy employees, in an effort to come together in a neutral space where everyone felt included. Our CEO Gold Bar declined and told me that the legacy Gold Bars and Gold Nuggets needed to join him, or they could see their way out as the others did. In his opinion, the prior beliefs and values of our organization were what contributed to its downfall. It was beyond clear that he did not respect the company, our science, or any of the Gold Bars and Nuggets that had poured their lives into it.

Over the next few months, most of the legacy Gold Bars and Nuggets did just that. They were not able to reconcile the differences between what had been and what now existed, and they were not willing to concede their beliefs and values. They did not trust the new Gold Bars, and they did not feel respected, supported, or heard. Several of the legacy Gold Nuggets and Bars did remain with the newly branded version of our company; however, most of us (including myself) left within the first few months.

The integration and rebranding of the company could have gone more successfully if provided with a space of understanding and respect as well as neutrality. We could have involved both sides in coming to a common ground that all could understand, where we did not have to necessarily agree, but at least to understand and be respected. This is not to diminish the new visions and brand, as that was never in question, but more about a neutral path to get there, which should have been a supportive, safe space involving both the newly hired Gold Bars and Gold Nuggets as well as the legacy Gold Bars and Gold Nuggets. Within that context, the organization may have been able to retain more of the legacy Gold Bars and Nuggets with the historical knowledge of process and procedure and the library of compounds that had yet to be moved into clinical trials.

The paradox of belonging and/or identity is critical when looking to foster a productive and successful working environment. When individuals feel like they belong, they are much more engaged, and this positively impacts productivity. Additionally, this sense of belonging yields loyalty and respect which provides Gold Nuggets and Bars who are willing and able to go the extra mile for their organization.

SCENARIO TWO

As we compare this experience with another one, the differences are immense.

I remember my first interview with two of the C-Suite Gold Bars. They had gotten me scheduled rather quickly, as they were in desperate need of an HR Gold Bar. I was blown away by their genuineness and how brilliant but nice and down-to-earth they were. The respect for each other as well as their work, the science, and even me was apparent. It had been so long since I had felt so welcomed, heard, and respected.

This was a small company of just over thirty Gold Bars and Gold Nuggets, but they were like octopi-people—by the amount of work they were getting done, surely they had to have at least eight arms each. It was the passion and sense of belonging that led to the formation of these working relationships and the ability of every Gold Bar and Gold

Nugget to go the extra mile and work outside of what was printed on their job description.

Respect and understanding were felt throughout the organization and even by our vendors and consultants. Trust was also a huge component of the company culture. We were fully remote and located throughout the world. The concept here…we trust and respect you to get your work done regardless of what time zone you live in, or are currently working in. We would plan activities for all to attend virtually and carve out minutes here or there where we spoke of our personal lives. We also had in-person meetings and an all-company trip as well so we could be together face to face.

The distance and time zones we had between us did not matter. The Gold Nugget and Bar working contributions never wavered, and the work always got done. We knew what our goals were, we knew what our tasks were, and we also knew what our deadlines were. Our Gold Bars trusted in our abilities to get it done successfully and on time, and so we did.

Prior to this company, I had never had the pleasure of working with or for an organization that not only promoted DEI&B but also lived it. It was the first time that female Gold Bars far outweighed the number of male Gold Bars. I had never seen that or experienced it in the past. Within the bulk of my career and experiences, we were lucky to have one female Gold Bar. A result of this was that there were no equity issues. As far as inclusion and belongingness, I felt that from the first interview, and it was even more ingrained with each passing day.

I knew within my first few weeks that I would stay with them as long as I possibly could, even until retirement, if that had been an option. But I also knew that their drug candidate was strong and had great clinical trials thus far. It wasn't long after I began working for my happy place that I sensed something was afoot. Sadly, I was right, and we were acquired by a large pharmaceutical company. But this wasn't bad news. This was amazing news for the company and a true success story in our industry. However, for those like me who just loved their job and their company, it was a sad day. I stayed on for another year through the transition and acquisition but then had to move along.

When comparing this transition with the prior case, it was like night and day. Through this acquisition we were terminating 100% of staff. Everyone was given the chance to review open positions with the large pharmaceutical company and apply for those, but outside of this, all employees would be terminated. Despite the message that could be perceived as doom and gloom, it was not felt that way. There was transparent and frequent communication between both organizations. We held regular informative meetings with both our company as well as members of the acquisition team on the pharmaceutical company's side. In addition, we supplied resources including FAQs, guidebooks, and weekly newsletters so that our transitioning employees could access information that they might have questions on 24/7.

Additionally, regardless of the level and position, everyone was treated with respect. There was a sense of empathy from the pharmaceutical's side, and that made it much easier to not only work with them, but also ask those "dumb questions" that people often think they have. During our transition time, we were encouraged to access and use their resources including things like continuing education, joining teams, and even all-company meetings and town halls. In our case, while we knew our time was ending, we were never treated as such, and this was key to a successful transition.

With these examples and cases, you can see how far simple fundamental concepts like respect, understanding, and empathy can take you. The foundations provide positive feelings and an overall sense of peace that comes from working in a respectful environment that values its Gold Bars and Gold Nuggets and trusts them to do their work. No price tag can be put on these measures, and what's more, they are free for the organization to enact, and yet pay off exponentially when it comes to productivity and, as a result, profitability.

CHAPTER NINE

THE END GOAL

The erosion of fundamental basics, including respect, empathy, and understanding, did not happen overnight, nor can it be repaired overnight either. The degradation of respect in our workplace has been building over years and years, maybe even decades, and our friend COVID-19, in all of its glory, brought those issues to the forefront. My point throughout this book is not about the doom and gloom but instead about preparedness. It's about the small, generally cost-free changes we can make to address this and prevent it from happening again in the future.

Certainly as I write, COVID-19 has shifted to be in our rearview mirror. However, I'm sure, like myself, you can remember the days when we would read ever-changing headlines and awake to new numbers and restrictions daily.

The reverse was also true when those restrictions were lifted. I remember articles in *The Wall Street Journal* about yet another shutdown in China or other locations. As the restrictions were lifted in the U.S., it was not because COVID-19 was over or the threat was done, it was just simply that the tolerance to handle such proactive measures has passed. Someday there will certainly be another massive shift, a new COVID-19 if you will, as there have been other pandemics throughout history. Our focus needs to be on the lessons learned from these experiences and how we can prepare for future events, so we are more successful in navigating both the event and the aftermath. We will definitely not win any awards within our workplaces for the handling of COVID-19, given the impact it has had on our workforce.

Being proactive versus reactive is an absolute key to success. You do not want to wait for the shit to rain down. You want to have some sort of plan or tool chest to protect yourself. Maybe you don't have a specific shit-centric umbrella in your arsenal. Even a generic umbrella will give you a head start in providing protection from future shit storms ensuing. We will never know exactly what is coming at us at any point in the future. However, shifting the culture of your workplace now will certainly prepare your team to gather together when shit begins to fall from the sky.

Preparing your team and your organization, Gold Nuggets and Gold Bars alike, is just like that. We have tools in our chest and can use them regardless of the shit storm that comes our way. I often tell my students, I could go through 345 different HR scenarios and what to do in all of them as your teacher, but it's number 346 that's walking through your door. So, my focus is not to be specific scenario-driven but instead tool and concept-driven so that you can apply them to any scenario that walks in, whether it's Gold Bar #753 or Gold Nugget #12. Regardless of what it is, you are proactive and have the tools and resources to handle those situations.

Let's now introduce to this mix a workplace filled with respect and empathy. This yields us a safe space where Gold Bars and Nuggets are willing and able to share their thoughts, feelings, ideas, and techniques. This also yields transparency and respect. With these foundations already part of your culture, solving issues and dealing with the shit storms that arise will be much easier work.

Being proactive also involves looking inward as we all have biases, both unconscious and otherwise. We need to look at and address these issues to help us in repeating mistakes we may have made in the past as a result of those biases. To take it a step further, biases might be directed toward people or generations, or maybe it's even about tasks or how we handle certain problems. Regardless of what that is, being introspective to acknowledge, address, and change those behaviors will make us much better Gold Bars and Nuggets for today and in the future.

Flexibility is also a cornerstone of proactiveness. The only thing that is constant in our lives is change. In order to be successful, we need to be able to bend and flex. Think about the workplace ten years ago versus today. It is drastically different, and even if we look back five years, in most cases it's still very different. This is not like Silly Putty, where it will just go back into shape—this is a forever change, and you cannot undo the experiences that have happened and changes that were instituted into our lives. Nor are you able to erase our memories like they do in sci-fi movies. My point here is that flexibility is key if you want to be proactive and have a happy and engaged workforce.

SATAN'S CIRCUS STRIKES AGAIN

I'm going to need to take you back to Satan's Circus for this one. You just knew it was coming. As you know, I was mandated into the office five days a week against my wishes. I had been doing my job successfully with a hybrid situation before this. As luck would have it, after this mandate, I was involved in a car accident. No one was hurt, no one apart from my almost brand-new car, that is.

In Southern California we have a lot of transient folks who do some unsavory things from time to time. As I was driving home from Disneyland about 11 p.m. on a Sunday night, one such transient threw several large rocks off of the highway overpass. It was too late before I saw these, and my poor car was the recipient of three of them, one being literally embedded in my transmission from the force of the impact.

Again, we were fine, no cause for concern. And it could have gone horribly if one of them had hit the windshield.

If you recall our experiences through COVID, you are aware of the supply chain issues we were facing and how impactful this was in the car industry. This was true for both new cars and car parts for those of us needing a major repair. My car was literally gutted like a fish on the underside by two of these boulder landmines.

I provide this background so you have the full picture of where we are going next. My car insurance, like many, has a limit as to the amount of time a rental car can be covered. That time limit for me was exhausted quickly, and while I tried proactivity by taking the rental car back Friday evening and not picking it up again until Monday morning, I still was no match for the supply chain issues I was facing.

At one point I had asked my Gold Bar if I was able to work remotely for a few days to help save time on this effort and was given a quick, "No." Um, okay. So onward I went and kept at it. Shortly after a few months of this, I was now liable for 100% of this rental car. It was $70 per day, and this was the insurance discounted rate, and I was having to pay this just to get to work and home again. So, as you can imagine, again I asked and again I was told, "No." I was literally paying $70 per working day, five days a week, to drive to and from work. This was on top of gas and all of the other anxiety and stress that come with normal life.

I will admit, there was one week when I was given a green light and able to work remotely for three days. But my point here is to say that it had already been proven that I was able to do my job remotely, I had extenuating circumstances, and I was in a desperate place. *No, no…just pay that ridiculous bill every week just so you can drive here.* My memory was not and will not be erased from the time I was successfully working remotely—when I was more than capable and had been doing my job remotely even within a hybrid model in the past for Satan's Circus. At the very least, I was just asking for a few days' reprieve from those car rental bills.

Within this period of time, my productivity was shit, my engagement was less than shit, and I spent most of my days on Zoom calls or sitting in my office staring at a wall wondering how in the fuck I had gotten here. If my Gold Bar had allowed for some flexibility in letting me work remotely while my car was being repaired, it would have positively impacted my happiness and productivity. I would have been grateful for their understanding, empathy, and respect. Instead, it fueled a fire of *how the fuck could you treat employees like this, Gold Bars or Nuggets?* Sadly, this situation led to a several-month solid depression. I had never felt so at a loss, completely out of control of my own life. The impact of this was immense and completely avoidable.

BUILDING YOUR FOUNDATION

Change is constant. The workplace for a Gold Bar who started twenty years ago is not today's workplace, and we need to have flexibility to edit and pivot some of those older workplace ideals to better match the demographics and needs of today's workforce. Older ideals that often placed work first will not be successful, as they will not attract and retain qualified, engaged staff. Instead, it will attract Gold Bars and Nuggets who need a paycheck now, or are desperate for an opportunity, or possibly biding time until a better job comes along.

Additionally, we need to equip our Gold Nuggets with information about the generational differences that parlay into our workplace expectations and values. With this information, our Gold Nuggets can better understand where everyone is coming from and can result in a two-way conversation, enabling a place of understanding. In the end, and whatever the reason, the effort you exert is going to be the effort you get back. So a sharp-assed comment or roll of the eyes will never yield you engaged employees, nor will these be the employees to get you through the tough times and struggles that are inevitable in our workplaces.

I hope that at some point throughout your childhood you were playing with LEGOS®—maybe even into adulthood. I will respectfully plead the fifth on this one for myself. (And if you only had Mega Bloks, I'm really sorry; these are, at least in my opinion, a lesser brick.) Anyone who has played with LEGOS knows that to build a strong foundation, you need that large, thin, flat base. In my day, that piece was a green baseplate, item #11023. Like any LEGO aficionado, I treasured that base plate and I used it for all of my building foundations. Gold Nuggets from different generations may have gotten to use a different color, but the principle is the same. In order to build a sound, strong-ass structure, you need to be smart about what you choose to use at the bottom.

When we talk about the re-entry of respect and empathy into the workplace, we are pulling out green baseplate #11023. We are adding this sound-ass structure to our corporate culture, and then being able to build to our heart's desire on top of that. But that base, those concepts of understanding, are fundamental in the overall success of that structure.

Situations like natural disasters, 9-11, and COVID-19 are going to continue to impact us, so it's imperative that we learn these lessons now from our current and past experiences and start changing that course for future events. When preparedness and proactiveness are the baseplate of your company culture, no matter what happens in the future, you will yield higher rewards, productivity, and profitability. You are ready because you have built a strong, steady foundation.

We need to be able to address and incorporate the values and mitigation techniques discussed within this book that support and encourage a workplace flourishing with respect, empathy, and understanding. With all of the generations currently in our workforce as well as the generations yet to come, we need to act now to correct our workplace values. Additionally, it is so important to be able to have our Gold Bars flexible and proactive in paving the way for successful Gold Nuggets on their road to becoming tomorrow's Gold Bars. The more these challenges are ignored, the worse the relationship strain becomes within our workplaces for both our Gold Nuggets and our Gold Bars. As Cher taught us all, you cannot turn back time. It was here, it happened, and we need to be able to accept it and move forward from it within our workforce.

CONCLUSION

As we have explored, we now know that both our Gold Nuggets and our Gold Bars bring equal treasures to the table. Both must be acknowledged and appreciated for their offerings. We look to our Gold Bars for lessons learned, experiences, and knowledge within our business and industry. They are leaders and have a wealth of wisdom to share with our Gold Nuggets so they can one day become the leaders and keep progress in a forward motion.

Our Gold Nuggets bring a more human approach and element to the table. They want to not only serve themselves and their families, but their communities and humanity overall. This is an incredible feat and should be cherished by all that surrounds it. Our Gold Bars can learn extensively from this application and add some aspects to their current practices to make our workplaces better and our workforces happier and more productive.

Sometimes opposing values cause conflict, but it is not about who is right and who is wrong. The focus needs to be upon offering a safe space filled with respect and empathy, where all parties feel comfortable sharing ideas, values, and suggestions for making our workplaces better.

Post-COVID has offered one of the clearest examples of value-based conflict. In truth, life cannot and will not return to pre-COVID working conditions. The landscape has changed too much. Instead of both sides stomping their feet, pounding their fists, and having a workplace tantrum, Gold Bars and Gold Nuggets should come together and imagine a new and better workplace that meets everyone's needs.

None of us have the ability to undo what COVID did, none of us have the ability to go back in time. (I mean, that I know of at least. I used to watch *Quantum Leap*, so there's that.) Regardless, today needs to be about acceptance and learning from these changes and experiences—creating spaces of proactivity with flexible and progressive movement forward in both the interests of our Gold Nuggets and our Gold Bars.

We are only successful if we are proactive and flexible. We must re-frame our mindsets to nurture relationships based on respect and empathy to shift our corporate culture for the better. As a result of this storm preparation, our employee engagement will rise, and both productivity and profitability will also increase, financially benefiting the company or organization. Gold Bars and Gold Nuggets who feel understood will be more loyal and put substantially more effort into everyday work, directly impacting the bottom line. In short, we are successfully batting down the hatches and navigating our way through this shit storm to actually come out into a better workplace for everyone.

We are not reinventing the wheel—instead we are bringing an awareness and a reminder of how we all want to be treated. We are the Gold Bars and Gold Nuggets working in today's workplace, and we deserve to be treated as such. We are not inmates in the asylum, nor are we children on the playground. So those mentalities need to stop and, honestly, should have stopped decades ago. Foundational elements of respect, understanding, and empathy will be repaid to the company through profitability if provided to our Gold Bars and Nuggets as part of the company culture.

Imagine a workplace where everyone works together and where everyone feels heard and appreciated, regardless of Gold Bar or Gold Nugget level. Now, fill that space with respect, empathy, and understanding. This could be your workplace and would be a space that you actually wanted to be part of, wanted to see succeed, and wanted to give your all to!

I wish you all the absolute best of luck in your Gold Bar and Gold Nugget adventures. I hope you are able to make the most of every experience and reach for your dreams wherever and whatever paths those may take you on. Thank you for exploring the Old West and panning for gold with me. May you find the gold purity that you are all looking for!

APPENDIX

This appendix is designed as a short-cut and quick visual for all of the areas we have discussed within this book. If you are like me, and just want to get to the heart of the matter, this is your section. For others, if you are truly wanting to better your workplaces, you can use this section as a checklist of the areas to be discovered on your journey to a happy, productive, and inclusive workplace. Respect and understanding yield dynamic, successful relationships that foster productivity and happiness in our workforce. Let this appendix be your guide on that workplace path.

WHAT HAS LED THE CULTURAL LANDSCAPE OF OUR WORKPLACES TO SHIFT:

- **Multigenerational Workplaces**
  - For the first time in history, we have five generations in our workplaces today—each possessing their own needs, wants, values, and differences
- **COVID-19**
  - Introduced a new way of working for a large majority of Americans
  - Changed expectations of the workers as related to working locations and connectivity
- **Role of Technology**
  - Multipronged:
    - Constant contact, or expected constant contact, because of the ease and accessibility of technology
    - Social media, both within work and for those seeking new roles
    - AI, while still in the infancy stages, will most certainly yield drastic shifts in our workplaces
- **The number of workers with college degrees has increased greatly over the past decade**
  - Shifting the composition of those we have in the workplaces and thusly increasing those expectations

- **Company culture**
  - The inclusion of Diversity, Equity, Inclusion, and Belongingness (DEI&B) has drastically shifted our workplace ideals and expectations when compared with a decade ago

STRATEGIES FOR RELATIONSHIP BUILDING:

In all cases when we are talking about building and fostering these relationships, we are talking about the act of establishing a basis and then cherishing or nurturing that relationship to a happy and healthy place.

- **Basic fundamentals to help build and foster successful relationships:**
  - Respect
  - Empathy
  - Understanding
- **Tools to help build and foster successful relationships:**
  - Communication
  - Active listening
- **Values to be aligned to help build and foster successful relationships:**
  - Diversity
  - Equity
  - Inclusion
  - Belongingness

RESOURCES:

- **Mental Health**
  - Information regarding any applicable benefits such as EAPs or similar
    - Employee Assistance Programs or Plans
  - Creating a workspace and culture that is inclusive of mental health
    - Information readily available—not just upon hire
    - Speaking about it and folding it into the organization's culture
    - Listening to employees when coming to you with concerns or issues
    - Community
  - Community can come in many forms; consider the following:
    - Look to local geographical community resources to post or share with your organization
    - Find and share industry-specific resources and non-profit organizations
    - Additional community resources may tie directly to an occupation, such as the Society for Human Resource Management (SHRM) within HR
- **Support Groups and Information**
  - Support and educational information to share with your organization can come from a multitude of resources

- Benefit specific: tied to the organization's benefit programs and plans
  - If one must be eligible, be sure to specify what that eligibility is so employees would easily be able to assess if they could use the benefit or not
- Brokers and other business relationships
  - Benefit brokers and other possible contracted businesses may have support and resources available to you and your organization's employees
- Community
  - Local support groups, as well as industry or occupation specific groups, could have information and resources that you are able to share with all of your organization

ENDNOTES

1) "The Future of Time: A Study Fielded by Adobe Document Cloud," 2022, https://www.adobe.com/dc-shared/assets/pdf/acrobat/business/resources/future-of-time-hybrid-worklplace.pdf.

2) Mark Terry, "Reports: Odds of Getting Drugs to Market Range From 6% to 40%," BioSpace, April 30, 2019, https://www.biospace.com/never-tell-me-the-odds-what-are-the-chances-of-drugs-getting-to-market.

3) Branka Vuleta, "32 Mind-Blowing Biotechnology Statistics," Seed Scientific, October 22, 2021, https://seedscientific.com/.

4) Apollo Technical LLC, "Statistics on Remote Workers That Will Surprise You," June 18, 2024, https://www.apollotechnical.com/statistics-on-remote-workers/.

5) "How Does Gen Z See Its Place in the Working World? With Trepidation," McKinsey & Company, October 19, 2022, https://www.mckinsey.com/featured-insights/sustainable-inclusive-growth/ future-of-america/how-does-gen-z-see-its-place-in-the-working-world-with-trepidation.

6) Katherine Haan, "Remote Work Statistics and Trends in 2024," *Forbes Advisor*, June 12, 2023, https://www.forbes.com/advisor/business/remote-work-statistics/.

7) Mental Health in the Workplace, "Mental Health Disorders and Stress Affect Working-Age Americans," cdc.gov, July 2018.

8) "Belonging," Deloitte Insights, n.d., https://www2.deloitte.com/us/en/insights/focus/ human-capital-trends/2020/ creating-a-culture-of-belonging.html.

9) Paige McGlauflin Paolo Confino, "Tech Layoffs Are Disproportionately Hitting HR and Corporate Diversity Teams," *SHRM*, December 12, 2023, https://www.shrm.org/executive-network/insights/ tech-layoffs-disproportionately-hitting-hr-corporate-diversity-teams#.

10) Kristie Rogers, "Do Your Employees Feel Respected?," *Harvard Business Review,* June 21, 2018, https://hbr.org/2018/07/do-your-employees-feel-respected.

11) "Belonging," Deloitte Insights, n.d., https://www2.deloitte.com/us/en/insights/focus/ human-capital-trends/2020/creating-a-culture-of-belonging.html.

12) Christiana Torres, "The Business Case for DEIB in the Workplace," *Degreed Blog*, December 10, 2021, https://blog.degreed.com/the-business-case-for-deib-in-the-workplace/#:~:text=When%20an%20organization%20has%20a%20strong%20DEIB%20culture%2C,81%25%20more%20likely%20to%2-0indicate%20high%20customer%20satisfaction.

13) Jessica Rodell, "Volunteer Programs That Employees Can Get Excited About," *Harvard Business Review*, January 21, 2021, https://hbr.org/2021/01/volunteer-programs-that-employees-can-get-excited-about#:~:text=Many%20studies%20have%20shown%20that,and%20improve%20

ACKNOWLEDGMENTS

I have to begin this section with Kevin Munkholm. Kevin, we were just meeting for lunch to catch up—never did I expect a life-altering path to take shape as a result of a random thought flying out of my mouth too fast for me to stop it. At the time, I was miserable and salty. This poor attitude was a result of my job at Satan's Circus. I randomly, and very briefly, mentioned the idea of writing a book at lunch…enter Kevin as Father Christmas with the support, answers, and connections to make this possible. His introduction to Krista Clive-Smith has been a true gift. Kevin, you are brilliant, and I'm forever grateful!

Krista Clive-Smith, thank you for paving the road and creating a space where authors like myself can bring their ideas to life! You believed in me at a time when I needed it most. Next, and part of the KCS family, is Kelly Cleeve.

Kel, I can never thank you enough for being with me the entire way! The support, therapy, editing, and overall understanding have meant the world to me. You are the reason we get to finally put this puppy to print. Thank you both immensely!!!

Parents and close family can take many forms, and I want to thank you all! My mom, Uncle Nasty/Martha with the entire Withee Crew, Penna Ave, and of course Melon 3.0 and Egg. You have all been there listening to me bitch. I'll love you all! (Yes, it's "I'll love you" on purpose.) To Crispy Cream, you are forever in my heart, and I miss you so fucking much! I will never disappoint as your "Wayward One."

And obvy…with a book based on work shit, I cannot neglect to mention all of my work Peeps over the years. MJ, I would never trade our working days together for anything, and I cannot fathom a life without you in it! A million thanks for always being there and always listening!

More fun with work people without whom I would not be writing this: Ems Cat the Superhero and our crew of Clinical Cats, the legit Sewer Cats who I fed for years at Arena, Cunt Wiper, Narnia, Roy Boy, Brucey, Christie, and my beer peeps whether it was the Thursday night crew or a random beer gathering. Bean, you are such an amazing person, and I'm so proud of the HR professional you have become! Thanks to Laura and Hugh for doing it the right way, and finally, thanks to my Snooze girls. I know there are at least a few who I have not thought to mention, so please accept this as your accolade. Again, a million thanks to you all for the laughs, material for this book, and for your support in times of overall fuckery.

Mahalo, bitches!

ABOUT THE AUTHOR

Allison is a seasoned human resources professional with over 25 years of experience, bridging the gap between HR and organizational success. Currently pursuing a doctorate degree at Vanderbilt, she is fervently committed to shaping the future of HR. Allison lives on the east coast with her cat and dog.

www.ingramcontent.com/pod-product-compliance
Lightning Source LLC
Chambersburg PA
CBHW030521210326
41597CB00013B/988